The Institute of E
Studies in Biology no. 18

Population Dynamics

by Maurice E. Solomon

M.Sc., F.I.Biol.

*Reader in Zoology and Head of Zoology Section,
Long Ashton Research Station,
University of Bristol*

Distributed in the United States by
CRANE, RUSSAK & COMPANY, INC.
347 Madison Avenue
New York, New York 10017

First published 1969
by Edward Arnold (Publishers) Ltd.,
25 Hill Street,
London, W1X 8LL

Reprinted 1970
Reprinted 1971 (twice)
Reprinted 1973

Boards edition ISBN: 0 7131 2247 1
Paper edition ISBN: 0 7131 2248 x

Printed in Great Britain by
The Camelot Press Ltd, London and Southampton

General Preface to the Series

It is no longer possible for one textbook to cover the whole field of Biology and to remain sufficiently up to date. At the same time students at school, and indeed those in their first year at universities, must be contemporary in their biological outlook and know where the most important developments are taking place.

The Biological Education Committee, set up jointly by the Royal Society and the Institute of Biology, is sponsoring, therefore, the production of a series of booklets dealing with limited biological topics in which recent progress has been most rapid and important.

A feature of the series is that the booklets indicate as clearly as possible the methods that have been employed in elucidating the problems with which they deal. Wherever appropriate there are suggestions for practical work for the student. To ensure that each booklet is kept up to date, comments and questions about the contents may be sent to the author or the Institute.

1969   INSTITUTE OF BIOLOGY
                                              41 Queen's Gate
                                              London, S.W.7

Preface

This booklet is intended to give an introduction to population dynamics. The subject is concerned with a series of inter-related topics: (1) the numbers of individuals making up the population of particular species in specified places; (2) the changes in these numbers that are observed over a period and the differences in abundance in different places; (3) the rates of reproduction and mortality, and of gains or losses by dispersal, which together account for the changes in numbers; (4) the operation, singly and in combination, of the various factors influencing these processes of gain or loss— the effects of weather and other environmental factors, the effects of natural enemies and disease, and the effects of food shortage, crowding etc.; (5) the processes within the population as it reacts to this complex of influences both external and internal; and (6) the relative importance and the interaction of (i) processes that tend to regulate abundance and (ii) those that simply change it.

This is a complex and lively branch of biology, and is important for the control of pests, weeds and harmful animals, for the husbandry of domestic animals and crops, for the efficient use of fisheries, for the conservation of the countryside and its fauna and flora, and for the understanding and control of changes in human populations.

Long Ashton, Bristol, 1969   M.E.S.

Contents

1 Characteristics of Populations   1

1.1 What is a population?   1.2 Population of what?   1.3 Numbers, dispersion and density.

2 Aspects of Population Dynamics   4

2.1 What is population dynamics?   2.2 Questions in population dynamics.   2.3 Theory and reality.

3 The Functioning of Populations: Gains and Losses   8

3.1 The power of increase.   3.2 Mortality.   3.3 Dispersal. 3.4 Assessing rates of increase.   3.5 Population growth curves.

4 The Functioning of Populations: Fluctuation and Regulation   16

4.1 Fluctuations and cycles of abundance.   4.2 Regulation of abundance.   4.3 Regulation and density-dependence.   4.4 Factors, processes and density-relationships.   4.5 Non-regulatory processes.   4.6 Comparison of three basic density-relationships. 4.7 Population and environment as a working unit.

5 Population Interactions   32

5.1 Types of interaction.   5.2 Forms of density-dependence. 5.3 Interactions of predators and prey, or parasites and hosts. 5.4 Competition and self-regulation among higher animals.

6 Plant Population Dynamics   40

6.1 Similarities and differences between plant and animal populations.   6.2 Density effects and competition among plants.   6.3 Regulation of plant populations.

7 Economic and Social Population Problems   46

7.1 Crops as populations.   7.2 Populations of pests.   7.3 Biological control of pests.   7.4 The impact of modern insecticides. 7.5 Integrated control and pest management.   7.6 Man as a predator.   7.7 Populations of domesticated animals.   7.8 Human populations.

Exercises   57

References   59

Characteristics of Populations 1

1.1 What is a population?

Although we all use the word 'population', or perhaps because of this, it is
not easy to arrive at a strict and clear definition. Usually, a population is
taken to be a group of organisms of one species (although one sometimes
meets the phrase 'mixed-species population'). The group is usually sepa-
rated in some degree from other groups of the same species, by geogra-
phical or topographical barriers (as on an island, or in a lake, or under a
solitary stone), or by some boundary chosen by the investigator, who may,
for instance, consider the codling moths in a particular orchard, or the
frogs of a particular valley.

Some populations are clearly isolated and distinct, e.g. that of a species
of lizard on a remote island. Some, through being for a long time completely
cut off from other populations of their own kind, have evolved physical
differences from the rest of the species: for example, the short-tailed vole
has different forms, judged to be sub-species, on the islands of Eigg, Muck,
Islay and Gigha. Many animals and plants have a patchy distribution,
occurring in an irregular pattern of clumps and gaps. If the gaps are wide
enough, the clumps can be treated as populations.

Of course, the clumps may be only temporarily separate. Each infested
cabbage, and each cabbage field, may seem for a time to have its own population of cabbage aphis. But in the first place such colonies are set going by
winged aphids borne on the wind and settling on the plants. Then, as each
colony increases, it produces winged individuals which in turn take to the
air as potential colonists. Not only are the local colonies temporary, their
winged offspring mingle with aphids coming from other colonies.

Some animals tend to remain together in crowds during their wander-
ings, like schools of fish or swarms of locusts (Plate 1). It is safe to assume
that such groups, if they survive long enough, will intermingle with others
of the same species.

If we know that a population in a particular area has been separate over a
long period from others of the same species, it may seem appropriate to
study it as a whole. But this may not be practicable. We may have to confine
our attention to the part of it that we find in a particular valley or wood. We
may call this part of it 'the population of' our selected place. But we must
bear in mind that our boundary is not an absolute barrier, and try to
measure the rate at which individuals pass out of or into the area of study.
When we set about assessing the gains and losses to the population by
births and deaths, we have to count in, or allow for, these other gains and
losses from immigration and emigration.

So, although we may have a clear mental picture of an ideal population,

I

in its entirety and separateness, in practice we usually have to deal with a set of animals or plants that really forms only a section of such of an ideal population, and which is not entirely separate from the larger population of the surrounding region. We shall be fortunate if it forms some sort of recognizable natural unit, and is separate most of the time from the surrounding members of the species. In any case, it is convenient, and usual, to refer to it as 'the population' under study.

1.2 Population of what?

To understand the biology of a population, we obviously need a knowledge of the biology of the individuals comprising it. Primarily, we should know the characteristics of the species concerned; we may then go on to enquire whether the members of the population under study differ individually or as a group from those in other populations of the same species.

Besides being aware of obvious features such as the size, shape, lifecycle, habits and behaviour of the organisms concerned, we may, according to the aims of our study, need to learn something of their physiology under the conditions in which the population is living, or their genetic make-up and the genetic pattern of the population as a whole. For various, often compelling practical reasons, many population studies take no account of such matters, and some are seriously weakened by this deficiency.

The great majority of animal populations, and some of plants, include two different types of individuals, male and female. Their numbers are not necessarily equal. Since it is only the females that reproduce, the ratio of females to males (sex ratio) is a matter of significance.

Another source of internal diversity is that most populations include a mixture of individuals of different ages. When, as in human populations, individuals of all ages are present simultaneously, it is useful to know the relative numbers in successive age intervals, i.e. the 'age distribution' or 'age composition' of the population. Table 1 shows the age distribution in a human population (for brevity, the smaller age groups of the original table have been amalgamated).

1.3 Numbers, dispersion and density

In spite of the above remarks on the importance of biological characteristics, our primary concern in the study of population dynamics is with numbers. We nearly always require to know how many individuals make up the population, or alternatively what the population density is (e.g. average number of individuals per square metre of meadow or per cubic metre of lake water). Sometimes, when we attach importance to the difference in weight between young and mature individuals, we may prefer to use units of biomass, i.e. weight of organisms per unit area or unit volume of habitat.

Table 1   Age distribution of the home population of the United Kingdom, 1961, in thousands. Based on Table 7 in *Annual Abstract of Statistics*. No. **104** (H.M.S.O.)

Age groups (years)	Nos. in groups	% in groups
0–9	8,028	15·23
10–19	8,003	15·18
20–29	6,563	12·46
30–39	7,083	13·44
40–49	7,100	13·47
50–59	6,958	13·20
60–69	5,019	9·52
70–79	2,937	5·57
80 & over	1,017	1·93
Total:	52,708	100·00

If a population were spread uniformly throughout its habitat, a single figure for population density would apply throughout. But often the organisms are concentrated in certain parts, sparse or absent in others (uneven dispersion). Then the population density varies from place to place, so that the average density over the whole area may be an unrealistic guide to the effective density which the organisms experience.

The pattern of dispersion (or spatial distribution) of a population over the area it occupies is not usually regular. Even if the habitat is entirely uniform, which is seldom the case, and the members of a population are spread over it at random (i.e. as if the position of each one were determined by chance and were not influenced by the positions of its fellows), the pattern of dispersion will appear uneven in detail. Truly regular dispersion is to be seen in some plantations, such as that of the trees in an orchard, and is approached among certain animals or plants when they are of uniform size and closely packed together: sycamore aphids appear in a fairly regular pattern on a leaf by forming an aggregation, yet keeping each other 'at arm's length'. Most dispersion patterns, however, are not uniform, not even random, but show conspicuous clumps placed irregularly in a bare or sparsely occupied area. This may reflect irregularities of the habitat, reinforced by the reproduction of the organisms in the favourable spots; also, many animals tend to gather into groups, even on a uniform area. There are statistical methods for determining whether a dispersion pattern is more, or less, uniform than random.

The numbers in a population, or the density per unit area, are usually estimated by sampling, i.e. counting the numbers in small equal areas (etc.) selected at random. Clearly it is desirable to have a preliminary knowledge of a population's dispersion pattern when deciding on the size and number of the samples to be taken. On dispersion patterns and sampling, SOUTHWOOD (1966) or LEWIS and TAYLOR (1967) should be consulted.

Aspects of Population Dynamics 2

2.1 What is population dynamics?

If we say simply that population dynamics is the study of populations as functioning systems, this is true enough but it leaves far too much unexplained. This section will provide some further explanation.

In physical science, dynamics is the study of the behaviour of bodies under the action of forces that produce changes of motion in them. By analogy, the term population dynamics is applied to the study of changes in the numbers of organisms in populations and of the factors influencing these changes; also it includes the study of the rates of loss and replacement of individuals, and of any regulatory processes tending to keep the numbers steady, or at least to prevent excessive change.

The subject deals on the one hand with environmental influences upon populations, e.g. the effects of temperature and moisture, of the quantity of the food supply, of other species of organisms which compete for food or for other necessities, of natural enemies and of micro-organisms causing disease, and of various combinations of such factors. On the other hand it deals with the influence of members of the population upon each other, both favourable and adverse. The essential co-operative processes are those concerned with sexual reproduction and (in many species) the rearing of young. Also, members of a population may directly or indirectly protect each other to some extent from natural enemies, or against cold or other severe conditions, and they may modify the habitat to their joint advantage. Adverse influences may include competition for a limited supply of food, shelter or other requisites, mutual disturbance and fighting or even predation (cannibalism). External and internal influences may act in combination: e.g. adverse physical changes in the habitat may give rise to competition within the population for a few restricted refuges where conditions remain tolerable.

2.2 Questions in population dynamics

Although problems of population dynamics may occur to us in the course of spontaneous observations of nature, they arise much more often from our economic interests as hunters, fishermen, pastoralists, farmers or horticulturalists, and, nowadays, from our concern as conservationists. The following are a few examples of the questions that present themselves:

Why are some insects rather scarce and others abundant? What sorts of factors determine the difference?

What determines the abundance of rabbits, and how can their numbers be reduced?

Why is the shooting of wood-pigeons an ineffectual way of reducing their population in a region?

Why have red spider mite populations on apple trees often increased alarmingly when the trees have been sprayed to control codling moth?

Given a particular variety of wheat and type of soil and climate, what population density of plants will give the best yield per acre?

How much fishing will the North Sea herring populations withstand before being severely reduced, and what factors determine this?

At what level should whaling have been restricted to avoid putting various species in danger of extermination?

What is the best population density of sheep, or of cattle, on a given type of pasture, to secure the greatest annual yield of surplus animals that can be sold off?

How does the abundance of desert locusts depend on the weather, and how can we predict an outbreak?

Have the recent rapid increases in human populations been the result of increased birth rates or of reduced death rates, or both?

Some of these questions will be mentioned in later chapters, where the reader may find clues or even answers, and (more usefully) examples of ways in which such problems have been approached and solved.

2.3 Theory and reality

Answers to questions like those above may be suggested by close observation. However, natural conditions, or even those of agriculture or forestry, may be so complex that observations do no more than suggest hosts of possible explanations, or alternatively none at all. Experiments may be valuable as a means of putting proposed explanations to the test, but the results are often difficult to interpret unless many of the normally varying conditions have been stabilized. The practical investigation of population dynamics has been to a great extent concerned with ways of overcoming these difficulties.

Some biologists have preferred to study the dynamics of populations in the laboratory, where most of the variables can be kept constant. This is a flourishing branch of the subject, but two difficulties have arisen. The first is that we do not know how far we can apply the results of experiments under such artificially simplified conditions to the much more variable and complex situations in the field. This difficulty can in principle be overcome by gradually elaborating the laboratory experiments, making them larger and more complex, so as to bridge the gap between laboratory and field conditions. In practice this is a formidable undertaking, which has seldom been attempted. However, laboratory experiments have given us valuable insights into the dynamics of populations, and suggested ideas that may be tested in field experiments (by jumping the gap, rather than bridging it).

The second difficulty about laboratory experiments is that their apparent simplicity is often largely illusory. The more closely they are analysed, the more complex is the set of interactions revealed. Perhaps this is less a difficulty than a process of education.

Other biologists, or sometimes the same ones, have undertaken theoretical studies in which simplicity is guaranteed, at least in the early stages, because the whole exercise is conducted with very simple imaginary models of populations and their environments. Usually the study proceeds in mathematical form. What the theorist is doing is to use mathematical logic to find out the implications of the simple set of circumstances he imagined to begin with. This is deductive thinking, in contrast to the inductive approach of the man who makes observations on real populations and tries to discover explanations of the events he sees, by finding out what other events lead up to them.

There is no doubt that the theoretician has a much less laborious task that the practical investigator. His theory readily branches out in various directions, it can be systematically elaborated, it reveals surprising relationships that were not predictable offhand. He does, of course, need at least a modest command of algebra. But a crucial difficulty, regarded by some biologists as rendering theoretical studies largely valueless, is that the 'field' in which he operates is even more remote from reality out-of-doors than are laboratory experiments, and therefore we do not know to what extent his discoveries and conclusions apply in actuality. There is a good deal of truth in this: the initial assumptions which set the stage for a theoretical study need to be scrutinized very closely, and their validity tested against known facts or against new observations or experiments. On the other hand, theoretical studies have at the least provided stimuli of the first importance for the development of population dynamics. They have been a most valuable source of ideas to be tested in practice, and have provided starting points for a good deal of productive research.

Recent thinking favours the development of theoretical models and practical studies step by step together (HOLLING, 1963, 1964). Ideally, the procedure should be somewhat as follows. First, a simple model is written down, the assumption and relationships being based as far as possible on knowledge of particular populations. Then the assumptions and relationships of the model are tested in field studies, and modified if necessary. Practical work also supplies numerical values for various symbols (terms) in the algebraic model. The next step is to develop the model mathematically, to derive some of its implications. These in turn can be tested in practical work.

This sort of development produces increasingly complex models. Fortunately modern computers can often deal with the mathematics involved, especially if the model has been constructed with computer programming in mind.

The Functioning of Populations: Gains and Losses

3.1 The power of increase

Reproduction is characteristic of all species of organism. As pointed out long ago by Malthus, it is a multiplicative process. Reproductive adults normally replace themselves by a greater number of offspring. Under favourable conditions, this increase more than compensates for the deaths that commonly occur during juvenile development, and there is a net rate of multiplication.

If for a moment we ignore mortality and other losses, and consider the reproductive rate of surviving adults, this is often impressive. Many insects lay hundreds of eggs, many frogs and toads lay thousands, and some fishes, such as the cod, produce millions. Even allowing for mortality, very high net rates of multiplication may be observed: when reared under highly favourable conditions in the laboratory, the flour- or grain-mite can increase seven-fold in a week.

If conditions remained favourable for continued multiplication, the numbers reached would soon be enormous. One hundred grain mites would become 700 in one week, 4900 in 2 weeks, 34,300 in 3 weeks, and over 28 thousand million in 10 weeks. The last figure is unrealistic, because overcrowding would spoil the conditions for rapid increase before any such level was approached; but it illustrates the tendency towards population explosion inherent in the reproductive process. Even a doubling of numbers per year is equivalent to 1000-fold increase in 10 years, or 10-million-fold in 20 years.

In the 1920s, the American biologist R. N. Chapman proposed to call the maximum rate of increase, of which an organism was capable under the most favourable conditions, its 'biotic potential' (see CHAPMAN, 1931). This was imagined to be opposed and reduced under less favourable conditions by 'environmental resistance'. Environmental resistance included the causes of mortality, and conditions (such as crowding, food shortage, cold, etc.) which reduced the rate of reproduction. If Chapman had been more successful in the logical development of this electrical analogy, and had gone on to use real circuits to imitate population dynamics, he would have been the inventor of the analogue computer. In the event, the ideas of biotic potential and environmental resistance remained too vague to be of much practical value. Nevertheless, interest in the rates of increase that populations are capable of under various conditions has continued. Obviously, the rate at which a pest or a useful animal can increase is something which concerns the economic biologist.

3.2 Mortality

In population biology, 'mortality' strictly means the rate of death, e.g. 20 per cent dying per year (and 'natality' is the corresponding term for the birth rate); but it is often employed simply as a synonym of death, or deaths, and I follow the perhaps reprehensible custom of using it in both senses.

Alongside reproduction, mortality is the twin starting point for most studies of population dynamics. Broadly (allowing for fluctuations and dispersal) these two phenomena offset each other. In this context, 'mortality' is shorthand for 'pre-reproductive mortality'. It is not just deaths, but early deaths, which more or less counterbalance the effect of reproduction in most animal populations.

The pre-reproductive death-rate required to hold a population in check depends of course on its powers of reproduction. If an animal has equal numbers of males and females, and each female produces on average 20 young, the mortality required to prevent an increase in numbers is 90 per cent; if 200 young, then 99 per cent mortality; if 2000 young, 99·9 per cent mortality.

The mortality may be measured and expressed in various ways, for example as numbers dying per week or per generation, as percentage of the whole population per year, or as percentages of age-groups within the population per month, and so on. Demographers (students of human populations) deal in survival rates rather than mortality. Their procedure is to compose a table, starting with a convenient number of newborn individuals and showing how many of these would survive in successive intervals through the whole life span. This display of the 'age-specific' survival rate is commonly called a 'life table'. For human populations, such data (Table 2) are required for national statistics and by life insurance companies who wish to estimate their risks as precisely as possible. Corresponding tables are sometimes drawn up for populations of animals. Table 3 is for the spruce budworm in an area of Eastern Canada. The caterpillars of this moth feed on the leaves of conifers. The table illustrates features common to many life tables for animals. The life cycle is divided into a relatively small number of intervals, and these intervals are of unequal length, corresponding to recognizable life history stages. This is because of the laboriousness of estimating the numbers in wild populations by sampling, and the difficulty of determining the precise age of individuals. It is also convenient, as in Table 3, to begin with the average number of eggs laid per female—200 in this instance. This is an averaged, or mean, life table based on 10 years' observations. It gives a simplified, tidied-up version of the spruce budworm's reproduction, mortality and dispersal; in reality, the values, and consequently the abundance of the budworm, vary considerably from year to year and from place to place.

Table 2 Life table for U.K., 1964–66. From *Annual Abstract of Statistics*. No. **104** (H.M.S.O.) The lx column shows the numbers surviving at the beginning of each successive 5-year age interval, starting with 10,000 new-born infants. Column ėx shows the average expectation of life at these ages

Age X	Males		Females	
	lx	ėx	lx	ėx
0	10,000	68·2	10,000	74·5
5	9,742	65·1	9,798	71·0
10	9,719	60·2	9,783	66·1
15	9,699	55·4	9,770	61·2
20	9,651	50·6	9,751	56·3
25	9,599	45·9	9,728	51·4
30	9,551	41·1	9,699	46·6
35	9,494	36·3	9,659	41·8
40	9,405	31·6	9,595	37·0
45	9,258	27·1	9,489	32·4
50	9,013	22·8	9,324	27·9
55	8,595	18·8	9,076	23·6
60	7,915	15·2	8,713	19·5
65	6,819	12·1	8,157	15·7
70	5,513	9·4	7,306	12·2
75	3,935	7·2	6,049	9·2
80	2,345	5·4	4,385	6·8
85	1,051	4·0	2,504	5·0

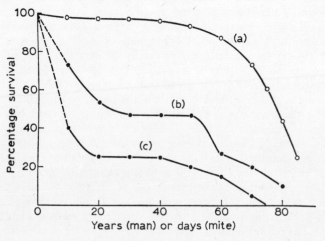

Fig. 3–1 Survivorship curves for females of man (curve (a), from Table 2) and of a predatory mite (*Cheyletus eruditus*) reared in the laboratory at 20°C, 65 per cent relative humidity (b) and at 25°C, 85 per cent R.H. (c).

Table 3   Abbreviated 'mean' life table for spruce budworm at Green River, New Brunswick, Canada (Modified from MORRIS, 1957)

Age interval (x)	No. alive at beginning of x (lx)	Factors responsible for mortality	No. dying during x (dx)	dx as % of lx (100 qx)
Egg	200	Parasites	10	5
		Other	20	10
		Total	30	15
Early larva	170	Dispersal	136	80
Later larva	34	Parasites	13·6	40
		Disease	6·8	20
		Other	10·2	30
		Total	30·6	90
Pupa	3·4	Parasites	0·3+	10
		Other	0·5+	15
		Total	0·9	25
Moth	2·5	Miscellaneous	0·5	20

Generation survival 2 (1 per cent)
Generation mortality 198 (99 per cent)
Sex ratio taken as 1:1 (equal numbers males and females)

In Fig. 3–1, the values for survival of females in Table 2 have been used to construct a 'survivorship curve' (a). Curves (b) and (c) in the same figure are based on corresponding data for a mite. The difference in shape is an aspect of the contrast between (a) a population with a relatively low reproductive rate, but high survival rate until towards the end of the life span, and (b and c) a population with very high reproductive rate but with rather heavy mortality in the early stages of the life span. Many examples of both types are known.

3.3   Dispersal

Many animals can fly, run or drift from their original habitat, and there is often a particular stage in the life cycle when they tend to do this. Sometimes the proportion that is lost by dispersal depends on the population density. More may be lost by dispersal than by death. In any case, dispersal losses are equivalent to mortality in the balance sheet of population numbers. Of course, dispersal may add individuals to the population as well as taking them away; these two processes are often referred to as immigration and emigration, although the word migration (without prefix) is more often applied to concerted directional movements like the flight of various birds southwards from northerly latitudes as winter approaches.

3.4   Assessing rates of increase

So long as the balance of gains and losses is positive, a population will be increasing. The practical work required in estimating the rate of increase is seldom easy; the degree of difficulty depends on the circumstances and on the level of accuracy required. Basically, the practical task is to estimate the numbers at intervals, usually by taking samples and counting the numbers in each. Complete censuses of populations are sometimes possible with the larger animals or plants, or with laboratory cultures. Fig. 3–2a is the graph of a series of estimates, each made on a different culture of mites;

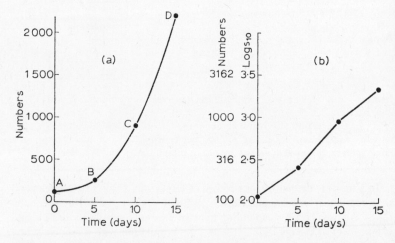

Fig. 3–2 (a) Observed increase of the mite *Acarus siro* in grain at 25°C, 80 per cent relative humidity. (b) The same data on a logarithmic scale of numbers.

a number of similar cultures had been set up simultaneously in the same way, kept under the same conditions, and taken out after various periods for estimation of the numbers of mites.

The calculation of the rate of increase from such estimates may be done simply enough. The net rate of multiplication (i.e. the geometric rate of increase) over any unit period is the number at the end of the period divided by the number at the beginning. In the three successive 5-day periods in Fig. 3–2a, the rates of increase are:

$$B/A = 258/118 = 2\cdot19 \text{ in 5 days}$$
$$C/B = 900/258 = 3\cdot49 \text{ in 5 days}$$
$$D/C = 2190/900 = 2\cdot43 \text{ in 5 days}$$

If we knew only A and D, and wished to calculate the mean rate of increase per 5-day period, we could call this mean rate x, and write:

$$D = Ax^3, \text{ whence } x = (D/A)^{1/3} = 2\cdot65$$

This is the same as a compound interest calculation, in which x would be the (constant) rate of interest.

A characteristic of steady geometric increase is that it generates a straight line slope when numbers are graphed on a logarithmic scale. The above population estimates are plotted on a logarithmic scale in Fig. 3–2b; the fact that the points are not precisely in line expresses the same deviations from a steady rate of increase as were shown by the above calculations. One might expect such variation to arise from uncontrolled differences between cultures, but in the present instance they also reflect real changes in the rate of increase. The rates of increase could be assessed graphically, by measuring the slopes of the lines joining the points in Fig. 3–2b. Rates of decrease could be assessed from a down-sloping line in a corresponding way.

It often happens that, instead of observing the increase of a population, we have data from rearing experiments. These may tell us how long, under a particular set of conditions, the animal takes to develop from the egg or new-born young to the reproductive stage, how many eggs or young are produced per female, and at what times in her life. If the reproductive period is much shorter than the developmental period, a simple calculation gives an approximate value for the rate of increase. Suppose, for example, an insect takes 3 months to develop to a short-lived adult stage, suffering 50 per cent mortality in the process, and laying, on average, 100 eggs between the 95th and 100th day of the female's life, with the highest number laid on the 97th day. We shall not be distorting the facts too much if we imagine all the eggs to be laid on the 97th day. Then if the sex-ratio is $1:1$, the daily rate of multiplication, x, can be derived as follows:

Start with 4 eggs, 2 male and 2 female.

After 97 days, one male and one female survive, and the female lays 100 eggs. Thus 4 eggs give rise to 100 eggs in 97 days.

Therefore $4x^{97} = 100$, or $x^{97} = 25$, or $97 \log x = \log 25$,

whence x (the daily rate of multiplication) $= 1\cdot034$.

The weekly rate of multiplication would be $x^7 = 1\cdot261$.

Values derived in this way might be applicable to, say, a mixed-age population of a stored-food pest under constant, uncrowded, conditions in the laboratory. (If we started with adults only, we should have a much higher rate of increase whilst they were reproducing, then no further increase until the offspring had grown to the adult stage. If we started with eggs, there would be no increase while the young developed, then a burst of multiplication by the adults, then another pause. These periodic waves of increase would gradually spread into a continuous process as the age composition of the population became more mixed.)

But with a field population in a temperate climate, the rate of increase would vary with the weather, food supply, etc. Also, the population might well be all of about the same age, and have only one or two generations in the warmer part of the year, remaining inactive over the winter. In such cases we should be interested chiefly in the rate of increase per generation, and in the influence of the current weather and other varying conditions upon this rate.

If an animal has an extended reproductive period, the above simple method of calculation is inapplicable. There is a relatively elaborate method of calculating the so-called 'finite rate of increase' (λ), which is the multiplication rate of a freely increasing population in which the proportion of individuals of various ages has settled down to a certain 'stable age distribution', characteristic of the population in the set of conditions concerned. The natural logarithm of λ is called the 'innate capacity for increase' (r). This represents the infinitesimal rate of increase in the differential equation $dN/dt = rN$, where N is the number of animals in the population. If N_t and N_{t+1} represent the numbers before and after a unit time interval, the relationship between λ and r can be expressed as:

$$N_{t+1}/N_t = e^r = \lambda, \text{ or } r = \log_e \lambda$$

($e = 2·718\ldots$, the base of natural or Napierian logarithms).

The method of calculating r from rearing data is described in the books by ANDREWARTHA and BIRCH (1954) and SOUTHWOOD (1966).

Another way of calculating the increase of a population, starting with a knowledge of the life cycle and the age distribution, is provided by matrix algebra. This method, and its application to examples in which a part of the population is periodically harvested, is explained by WILLIAMSON (1967).

3.5   Population growth curves

We have remarked that population increase cannot continue indefinitely. As the habitat becomes crowded, or as the exploitation of some essential requisite becomes more nearly complete, the rate of increase must diminish until the numbers reach a saturation point at which no further increase is possible. The overall curve representing increase from low numbers to saturation point is S-shaped (sigmoid) when a straight-forward arithmetic scale of numbers is used (cf. Fig. 3–3).

A well-known model of such population growth is the logistic or Verhulst–Pearl curve. This is a highly simplified model, based on the following assumptions: All the animals are effectively identical—at any

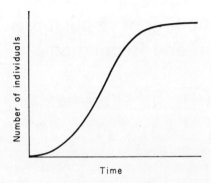

Fig. 3–3   A logistic curve of population growth.

particular time, all are equally likely to reproduce, and all equally likely to die; the rate of increase at any time depends only on the numbers present; when expressed in a certain way, the rate of increase is linearly proportional to the degree of unsaturation of the habitat, or to the difference between the saturation density and the density at the time. (Here we take density and numbers to be alternative ways of expressing the size of the population. Another way is to take biomass, the combined weight of all the individuals present.) Finally, it is assumed that the temperature and other environmental conditions are constant. From these assumptions the following equation can be derived:

$$\frac{\mathrm{d}N}{\mathrm{d}t} = rN\frac{(K-N)}{K}$$

where $\mathrm{d}N/\mathrm{d}t$ is the instantaneous net rate of addition to the population, r is the innate capacity for increase (cf. page 14), N is the number of individuals present, and K is the number the habitat can hold at saturation (so that the expression in brackets represents the degree of unsaturation of the habitat, as a fraction).

A more usual equivalent of this equation is:

$$N = \frac{K}{1 + e^{a-bt}}$$

where a and b are constants related to the steepness and height of the curve, and t is the time (on the scale along the x axis).

The logistic equation has been very widely used in the interpretation of population growth curves. It does not follow that the assumptions it is based on hold true in these cases: very often it is clear that they cannot possibly apply. For an analysis that is biologically realistic, other models of sigmoid curves must usually be developed, on the basis of assumptions appropriate to the case.

The Functioning of Populations: 4
Fluctuation and Regulation

4.1 Fluctuations and cycles of abundance

In the previous section we remarked the great power of increase inherent in many animals; on the other hand, disaster may strike suddenly and take a high proportion of the population. In consequence, many populations are subject to considerable fluctuations in numbers. Some fluctuate slowly, some rapidly, some strikingly and continually, others rather little, or at long intervals.

The causes of population fluctuation are many. Notably, with insects, they include seasonal and other changes in the weather, but also changes in food supply, and the attacks of natural enemies including the micro-organisms causing disease. Sometimes one particular factor can be identified as the chief cause of fluctuation in a population, and is referred to as the 'key factor'. Sometimes we can distinguish between immediate and under-lying causes of fluctuation. For example, weather may affect the numbers of aphids directly, by killing some of them, or it may affect them indirectly by altering the condition of the plants they feed upon.

A special type of fluctuation is seen in all animals (and plants) that have a reproductive period restricted to a particular season. There is then a periodic rapid increase by production of young, followed by a more gradual decline as death or dispersal reduces the numbers. Fig. 4-1 illustrates such a case.

Usually we are more concerned with the less regular fluctuations in numbers caused by environmental factors. In a seasonally reproducing population like that in Fig. 4-1, such fluctuations may be detected by com-paring the numbers at one particular stage of development in successive years (dashed line): here, the range of fluctuation in numbers of adult grasshoppers from year to year is approximately from 1000 to 3500. Fig. 4-2 shows the same phenomenon (inter-generation fluctuation) in a popula-tion of the pine beauty moth, as determined by estimating the density of the population of pupae in the ground at a site in Germany. On the arith-metic scale (solid line) we see a decline ending about 1925, and an out-break and decline around 1931; at other times the numbers were relatively low and seem rather steady. This steadiness is only apparent, as is seen when the numbers are plotted on a logarithmic scale (dashed line). Be-cause the logarithmic scale clearly displays fluctuations at low density, and keeps the great increases to a reasonable height on the graph, and for other reasons, it is widely used for plotting population figures, as here and in Fig. 4-1.

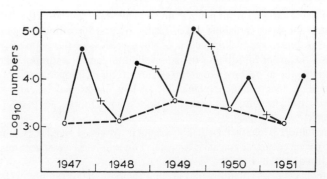

Fig. 4-1 Annual population cycle of the grasshopper *Chorthippus brunneus* on a site in Berkshire. ○ Adults, ● eggs, + nymphs. The dashed line shows fluctuations in numbers of adults in successive generations. (Based on RICHARDS, O. W. and WALOFF, N. (1954), *Studies on the Biology and Population Dynamics of British Grasshoppers*, Bulletin **17**, Anti-Locust Research Centre London.)

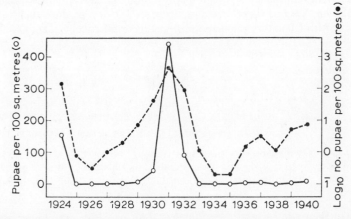

Fig. 4-2 Counts of pupae of pine beauty, a noctuid moth whose larvae attack the needles of Scots fir, at Neuendorf in Germany. Dashed line shows numbers on logarithmic scale. (Data of SCHWERDTFEGER, F. (1942). *Z. angew. Entom.*, **28**, 254–303.)

If we set out to study and interpret the changes in abundance of a population from generation to generation, an early step is to try to identify the 'key factor', which, as mentioned above, is the one responsible for the greatest proportion of the fluctuation. Here, it is the amount of change we are concerned with. We may find, for example, that differences in temperature account for more of the difference in abundance from generation to generation than does any other factor. In that case, temperature is the key factor. Other factors may cause a higher mortality, but so long as their effect is less variable from generation to generation than the effect of temperature, the latter remains the key factor. Such information is useful, not only as a step towards the analysis of the dynamics of the population, but also as a means of forecasting the trend of abundance (assuming there is a time lag in the appearance of some of the effects of temperature upon the population). Convenient explanations of key factor analysis, and of the methods used, are given by VARLEY and GRADWELL (1960), SOLOMON (1964) and SOUTHWOOD (1966).

Fluctuation is characteristically irregular. When a regular pattern appears, we often prefer to call it a cycle. The annual cycle of reproduction and subsequent decline (Fig. 4–1) is a case in point.

Regular cyclic oscillations that are not expressions of the life cycle have been depicted in theoretical studies by Lotka, by Volterra (see Appendix to CHAPMAN, 1931), and by NICHOLSON and BAILEY (1935). They were concerned with making algebraic models of the changes in numbers of hypothetical predators (or insect parasites) and their prey. It was calculated that the predators would reduce the numbers of their prey and in turn be themselves reduced by shortage of prey until the latter increased again, and so on. Various experimentalists have set out to reproduce such oscillations with laboratory populations of insects or other convenient animals.

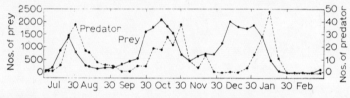

Fig. 4–3   Oscillations of a predatory mite, *Typhlodromus*, and its prey, a plant mite *Eotetranychus*, in a complex laboratory habitat (3 trays of oranges, with some paraffin barriers). (Based on HUFFAKER, C. B. (1958). *Hilgardia*, **27**, 343–83.)

One of the more successful examples is shown in Fig. 4–3. These oscillations have been called 'reciprocal', for they depend on the two-way interaction between the predators and prey.

Regular oscillations can be brought about in other ways also. The cause of oscillations between species interacting as above is the delay or persistence of the influence of one upon the other. This is suggested by the fact that cyclic oscillations can be induced in a single species by the delayed effects of competition for a continuous but limiting supply of food. NICHOLSON (1954) demonstrated this with populations of an Australian blowfly in cages in the laboratory (Fig. 4–4). In the example illustrated, the numbers of insects were restricted by the limited supply of food for the adults. When the flies were numerous, the shortage of food greatly reduced the production of eggs, so the number of flies later fell to a low level;

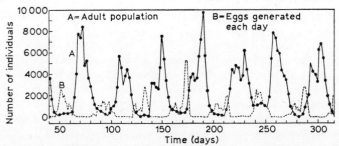

Fig. 4-4 Oscillations in numbers of a laboratory population of a blowfly, *Lucilia*, given ample food for the larvae but a limiting supply of only 0·5 g of ground liver daily for the adults. (Based on NICHOLSON, A. J. (1954).)

but then the supply of food was enough to enable what flies there were to produce numerous eggs, which developed to a large number of flies, and so on.

Some oscillations of predators and prey look regular enough, but seem not to be really reciprocal. In the north of Europe and Canada, lemmings and other mouse-like mammals fluctuate in a roughly 4-year cycle, and this is reflected in the numbers of their predators, such as the arctic fox and the snowy owl. The snowshoe hare of Canada fluctuates in a 9–10 year cycle, which is reflected in the numbers of its predator, the lynx. It is considered unlikely, however, that the predators are responsible for the cyclic changes in the numbers of the prey.

4.2   Regulation of abundance

We have remarked that populations may fluctuate irregularly in response to changes in weather or under the influence of other environmental factors. We may be tempted to think that whether they increase or decrease, and by how much, is a matter of chance, like the weather from week to week. But if this were the whole story, there would be nothing to prevent the fluctuations gradually or rapidly making the population more abundant, or less abundant; there would be nothing to prevent the 'ups and downs' drifting preponderantly in one direction or the other, until the population either died out or entirely overran its environment. Most populations that have been observed do not do this; although they change in abundance from generation to generation, over a period they tend to preserve a characteristic level of abundance, so that we can say a species is 'common' or 'rare' or 'very abundant' in a particular habitat, and if there are striking changes at times, so long as the habitat retains its essential features the animals generally return fairly soon to their characteristic abundance or scarcity (see Figs. 4-1, 4-2, 4-3).

Another consideration is the probability, and in many cases the observed fact, that, as abundance increases, there is a progressive building up of resistance; at least there appear drastic checks to further increase when the numbers rise above a certain level. For example, at high densities there may be a shortage of food, or the animals may continually disturb each other, or one of their natural enemies may exploit the large numbers better that it did the smaller ones. In one way or another, at a certain stage the further increase of the population is first hindered and then prevented, and finally the numbers may be forced down again (for example, if the food supply has been over-taxed, there may be a period of famine). Increasing penalties against rising density are the essential feature of the idea of 'regulation'.

If the increase of a population is to be limited in this way, there must be at least one adverse influence that comes into play more strongly when the numbers rise, and ultimately stops further increase. When the numbers decline again (through a persistence of the adverse influence that has stopped increase, or through an unfavourable change in some other factor, such as the weather), the adverse factor that was called into play by the rise in abundance often becomes less effective (if it does not do so, the population may be exterminated). Factors which operate in this way, becoming more effective at high population density, and less effective at low density, are called 'density-dependent'. There may be several such factors operating at different times or places, or at different levels of abundance, or all together, contributing to the regulation of population.

4.3 Regulation and density-dependence

Sometimes the inspection of a series of population counts will yield evidence of regulation. It may enable us to answer the questions: Does the proportional rate of increase decline when, or where, the numbers are high? Does the population decrease more often, and perhaps more rapidly, when numbers are high than when they are low? Is the rate of increase proportionately greater when numbers are low? Does the population in-increase more rapidly and/or more often when numbers are low?

In the field, even if we think we can detect such tendencies, there will be many exceptions to the general trend. There will also be false evidence, e.g. when the weather changes adversely at a time when numbers are high and produces effects which may be only partly, if at all, a response to high density. Therefore we require a long series of observations so that the regulatory trends may appear clearly through the non-regulatory fluctuations. We shall need statistical tests to show whether or not the apparent density-related trends have a significant probability of having arisen by chance.

Regulation, as we remarked, is a result of the action of density-dependent factors. (We shall see shortly that this way of putting the matter is somewhat inadequate, but it will serve for the present.) How can we determine whether or not a particular factor is acting in a density-dependent way?

The straightforward approach to this is to assess its adverse effect at different levels of population density or abundance. As an example we may take the case illustrated in Fig. 4–5. The animals concerned are the caterpillars of the winter moth; they feed on oak leaves and incidentally swallow

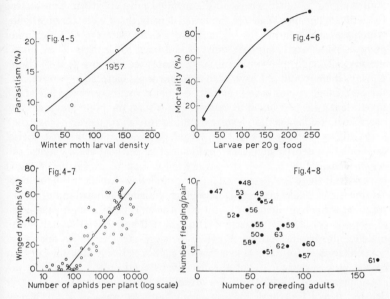

Fig. 4–5 Percentage parasitism of winter moth caterpillars by the parasitic fly *Cyzenis albicans* on 5 oak trees in Wytham Wood, nr. Oxford, 1957. (HASSELL, M. P. (1966). *J. Anim. Ecol.*, **35**, 65–75.)

Fig. 4–6 Mortality of caterpillars of the Indian-meal moth confined on 20 g of food. (Data of SNYMAN, A. (1949). *J. Entom. Soc. S. Afr.*, **12**, 137–71.)

Fig. 4–7 Percentage of winged nymphs (4th instar) of the cabbage aphid in relation to numbers on plants. At Canberra, Australia. (After CLARK, GEIER, HUGHES and MORRIS, 1967; courtesy of Methuen & Co. Ltd.)

Fig. 4–8 Breeding success of great tit in Marley Wood, nr. Oxford, in relation to number of breeding pairs present, 1947 to 1963. (After LACK, 1966; courtesy of The Clarendon Press.)

the eggs of a parasitic fly which lays them mostly where the foliage has been damaged. In a wood near Oxford, the entomologists Varley and Gradwell estimated the population density of the caterpillars on each of five oak trees, by collecting samples. They counted the proportion that contained parasites (which would ultimately kill them). The graph shows that where the caterpillars were more abundant, a higher proportion of them were parasitized, i.e. the parasite was acting as a density-dependent factor.

Before leaving this example, we may use it to illustrate some other notable features of density-dependent factors:

(1) It is not enough for the adverse effect to increase as population density increases: there must be a *proportional* increase in the effect. Fig. 4–5 shows that roughly 10 per cent were parasitized when the population density was 50, and about 19 per cent when the density was 150. This is of course a proportional increase in the incidence of parasitism. Considering the animals per unit space, at the lower density there were 50, of which 5 were parasitized, and at the higher density there were 150 of which 28 or 29 were parasitized. Suppose only 10 had been parasitized at the higher density; although this would still have been twice as many as at the lower density, there would not have been a proportional increase in parasitism— the percentage would have been only 6·6 per cent; there would have been no tendency for parasitism to increase faster than the population, so as to overtake it and, at a certain level, prevent its further increase.

(2) Fig. 4–5 shows us that the percentage parasitism continued to rise, as population density increased, up to about 22 per cent at the highest observed density (about 175). It does not tell us how much further it would have risen if there had been even higher population densities. We must not assume that it would necessarily have gone on rising as shown in Fig. 4–5 to reach, at some high density of winter moth caterpillars, a high value such as 80 or 90 per cent parasitization. It might well have been that there were not enough parasites, or not enough of their eggs, to accomplish this.

(3) It follows from the above that we cannot tell, from the information in Fig. 4–5, whether or not the parasite was effectively regulating the abundance of the winter moth, i.e. prevening its increase beyond a certain density. It was apparently making a contribution towards this, but it may have been necessary for other factors to finish the job. Thus, while regulation cannot be achieved without one or more density-dependent factors, it does not follow that every density-dependent factor is exercising regulation.

The adverse influence concerned in Fig. 4–5 is a form of mortality (parasitized individuals die before being able to reproduce). Fig. 4–6 illustrates another example in which mortality increases as density rises. This relationship is clearly seen in laboratory experiments, like the one illustrated, in which numbers of animals are confined in a small space with a limited food supply. The more crowded they are, and the smaller the share of food per individual, the higher the proportion that dies before maturity. Other consequences of such conditions may be smaller individuals and a reduced rate of reproduction. (A similar example is to be seen in Fig. 5–1.) In the study on which Fig. 4–6 is based, the experimenter did not determine the cause of the density-dependent effect—whether, for example, it was food-shortage or mutual disturbance. In the following examples also (Figs. 4–7 and 4–8), the only cause specified is increased population density, so that density-dependent factors are not distinguished. Very often in ecological work, the stage illustrated is reached first, and the more searching analysis of causes is attempted later.

Unlike the earlier examples, in which the adverse effect of raised density was increased mortality, the effect shown in Fig. 4–7 has to do with dispersal. Crowding increases the production of winged forms, which subsequently leave the plants.

The effect illustrated in Fig. 4–8 is of yet another kind: it takes the form of a reduction in the numbers of young birds successfully reared by each pair when the breeding population is high. If we were to make a graph of this *reduction*, it would be similar in orientation to the other examples of density-dependence we have seen. But the graph shows *performance*, which declines as density rises, so the trend of the points in Fig. 4–8 is downwards, instead of upwards as in Figs. 4–5 to 4–7. The effects of density become more severe as density rises, but performance, as reduced by these density effects, declines. Further examples of density-dependence expressed in this way may be seen in later sections (Figs. 5–2, 6–1b, 6–2).

The reciprocal predator-prey oscillations referred to earlier (Fig. 4–3) involve a special type of regulation. Although the numbers of predators and prey continually rise and fall, these changes are controlled and somewhat regular. Also, while the predator regulates the prey, it is itself regulated by the supply of prey. Each acts as a density-dependent factor upon the other. As we remarked earlier, the oscillations arise because of the delay or persistence of these density-dependent influences. Because of this, predators, insect parasites and the micro-organisms of disease have been called 'delayed density-dependent' factors. The name should be reserved for those actually involved in reciprocal oscillations; so far, such oscillations have been demonstrated chiefly in experiments; although they may be common under natural conditions it is not so easy to identify them with certainty.

4.4 Factors, processes and density-relationships

When we refer to a 'factor', we are using a convenient mental device to separate for special attention a particular aspect of the whole complex presented by a population in its environment. Any part or aspect of this complex can be regarded as a factor influencing the population, as, for example, predators, temperature, or mutual disturbance. The working of any influence upon the population is best referred to as a 'process': predators are a factor; predation, although we may refer to it as a factor, is more appropriately called a process. An aspect of the processes affecting populations is their density-relationship—whether, for example, they are intensified at high densities. A process that is affected in this or in some other way by the density of the population is 'density-related'.

The action of a density-dependent factor can be compared with that of the governor on an engine—a device which restricts the supply of liquid or fuel as the engine runs faster, and increases the supply as the speed falls. In cybernetics, such action is called 'negative feed-back'. In populations, we do not find the precision and repeatability that engineers demand, but the general idea is common to both fields.

Envisaging such simple and direct density-dependent action by a single factor, we may say that such a factor must be responsive to changes in the density of the population it acts upon. It must itself be influenced by this population density, just as the governor must be influenced by the speed of the engine if it is to regulate it. Processes generated by the population itself (e.g. competition for something, mutual disturbance) are inevitably and automatically density-dependent.

4.5 Non-regulatory processes

Having recognized the special features of those processes tending to bring about regulation, i.e. of density-dependent processes, we may consider the characteristics of some other sorts. Factors (or processes) that affect a population in a way which is unrelated to its density are called 'density-independent'. For example, if a proportion of the insects and spiders in a pasture are killed by the trampling of cattle, it is probable that the percentage affected will not depend upon whether these arthropods are sparse or abundant. (The percentage killed will of course depend on the population density of the *cattle*, and the *numbers* killed will depend on the population density of the arthropods as well as on that of the cattle, but neither of these relationships is relevant to the question of whether the cattle are a density-dependent factor for the arthropods.) It is not that a density-independent factor usually remains constant in its proportional effect while the density varies; it is much more likely to vary a good deal from time to time or from place to place: but so long as the variations in its influence are not significantly correlated with the variation in density, it remains density-independent. An example is illustrated in Fig. 4–9.

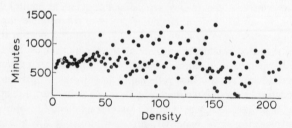

Fig. 4–9 A density-independent relationship: the length of a generation of the ciliate protozoan *Woodruffia metabolica* and its population density in a laboratory culture. (SALT, G. W. (1967). *Ecol. Monogr.*, **37**, 113–44.)

The effects of weather are often assumed to be density-independent, and no doubt this is very frequently true for all practical purposes. But, as we

have already noted, the effects of particular factors are commonly influenced by the effects of others. The weather itself is not influenced by
population density, but its effect may be. For example, the animals may
have been abundant enough to eat down the vegetation which would otherwise have provided shelter against rain or drought, so that few now survive
the downpour or the dry conditions. If they had been less numerous, their
shelter might have been preserved. Even if the animals have not damaged
their habitat in this way, if there are far more of them than the sheltering
sites can accommodate, the surplus will either move away or (as we assume
here) will be killed. The proportion that is killed by the severe weather
will depend on the abundance of the animals. Does this mean that the
effect of the weather is density-dependent? Only if we ignore the part played
by the limited supply of shelter. An inadequate supply of anything that is
needed by the animals has density-dependent consequences: the more
animals there are, the higher the proportion that must go short, or the
smaller is the share of each member of the population. Some ecologists
would say that the density-dependent effect is provided by competition for
the limited supply (competition being automatically density-dependent).
Perhaps the most satisfactory statement of the matter is that weather, the
capacity of the shelters, and the numbers of the animals jointly bring into
play a density-dependent process.

Besides density-independent processes, there is another type whose
effect is non-regulatory. This is the opposite of density-dependent, inas-
much as the adverse influence is proportionately *smaller* when numbers are
higher than when numbers are low. For example, predators or insect parasites often increase their rate of attack when the numbers of their prey increase, but not in proportion—the percentage attacked is less than before.
Fig. 5-3 (p. 36) shows that the parasite of a sawfly attacked more cocoons
when these hosts were more abundant, but the proportion attacked was
less, as shown by the fact that the curve turns towards the right. (It may be
shown more explicitly by reading off some approximate values from the
curve and converting to percentage of hosts attacked at two or more density levels.) This is an 'inverse' density-relationship; the proportional
effect of the factor is less at the higher densities. The *numbers* affected may
fall as density rises, or remain the same, or increase, so long as the *percentage* affected is less when density is high. This sort of relationship has
also been called 'density-disturbing', or simply 'disturbing'—the effect is
the opposite of regulatory.

Another example of an inverse density relationship is associated with
'under-crowding'. If a population is very sparse, its reproduction and increase may be hindered because the sexes meet too seldom for prompt
mating of the young females. In some circumstances this leads to a reduced
rate of increase. The adverse effect, which is analogous to a sort of mortality, of course becomes more severe as the density falls, or less severe as it
rises. To take another example, some animals need to modify their habitat

so as to adapt it better to their needs; the fewer the animals, the less effectively may they be able to do this. For instance, grazing animals maintain the grassland on which they thrive; this requires a certain 'grazing pressure' in order to prevent the natural reversion to scrub and woodland which otherwise occurs.

The alert reader will have noticed that in this last example, and perhaps also in the previous one, we are dealing with a *beneficial* effect associated with high (or not-too-low) density. Naturally, the lower the numbers the less the beneficial effect operates, and we treated this as an adverse effect of low density. He may prefer to regard these beneficial effects as examples of a separate sort of density-relationship. If he does this, the effects are still of course density-disturbing (though no longer inverse)—their effect is the opposite of regulatory, for they foster the increase of dense populations and hinder the increase of sparse ones. The latter characteristic is a dangerous one for populations at a very low density.

4.6   Comparison of three basic density-relationships

The essential features of the three major types of relationship discussed above—density-dependent, inverse, and density-independent—may be illustrated and compared in simple diagrams. In Fig. 4–10 the horizontal scales represent population density. The essence of the distinction between the three relationships is shown in (a). For simplicity, density-ndependence is shown as a horizontal line, although the scatter of points in Fig. 4–9 is more typical. In (b) the vertical scale is in simple numbers instead of in proportional terms; it might for example show numbers dying instead of percentage mortality. The consequences for the graphical form of the three relationships are as shown. In (c) the vertical axis has a scale of beneficial effects or positive aspects of performance. When these beneficial effects are expressed in proportional terms, i.e. effect or performance per individual, as in (c), we have a simple reversal of (a)—a reversal because density-relationships are defined in terms of adverse effects. If the beneficial effect or performance is expressed in straightforward numbers, e.g. as weight of the whole population, or total number of young produced, the interpretation of the forms of curves is still possible but not so obvious, and it is advisable to convert the performance or effects to values per individual, as in (c), or to calculate the reductions in performance, by subtracting the figures from the highest performance observed, and plot these differences as adverse effects per individual, in form (a).

4.7   Population and environment as a working unit

We have seen that populations are influenced by different sorts of factors, some density-dependent, some inverse, many density-independent. A population is not only influenced (by its own members, and by outside factors): it also influences its habitat and some at least of the other organisms sharing the habitat: therefore a population and its environment can be

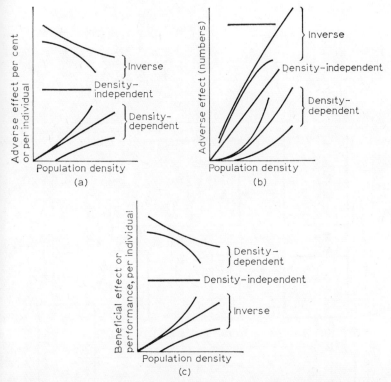

Fig. 4-10 Showing **(a)** the three basic density relationships, and the forms they take when **(b)** absolute instead of percentage (or per individual) values are plotted against population density, or **(c)** beneficial instead of adverse effects are plotted against population density.

seen as a single complex functioning entity—the 'ecosystem' (Fig. 4-11). However, for a particular population, there are usually many factors (including some of the other organisms) which seem to have no significant influence upon it, either directly or indirectly. In judging a particular factor to be irrelevant we may sometimes be mistaken; nevertheless, in a practical study, it is usually necessary to concentrate on the factors that appear to be significant and to ignore the rest, in order to keep the study within practicable bounds. The term 'life system' has been used for the entity comprising a population and the relevant items in its environment (CLARK *et al.*, 1967).

The elements in a life system are connected by a complex network of different influences. For example, a population may be influenced by various natural enemies, on which it also has an influence as a source of food, the environmental temperature may affect the various enemies as well as the population itself, thus modifying their interactions, and so on.

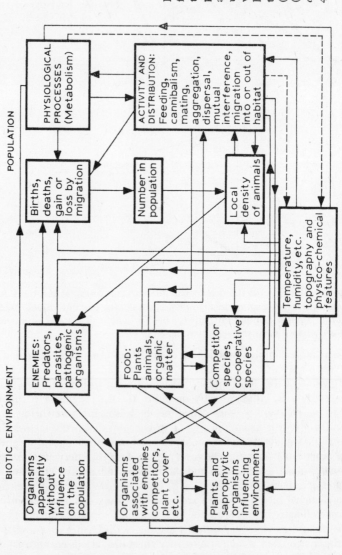

Fig. 4-11 Some influences, relevant to the dynamics of a population, within and between the population and its environment. Arrows lead from influent to influenced items. (SOLOMON, M. E. (1953). *Chem. & Industry*, **1953**, 1143–47.)

One consequence of these interacting influences is that accounts of the regulation of a population by a particular process, or of the degree of fluctuation caused by a particular key factor, are valid only for the set of conditions under which they have been tested. Under other conditions the outcome may be quite different. For example, populations of the grain mite *Acarus siro* are often reduced to the point of extinction by the predatory mite *Cheyletus eruditus*; but the degree of success of this predator in controlling its prey is very much dependent upon the temperature and humidity, and if these are not favourable it cannot prevent the increase of the grain mite. The temperature influences both predator and prey, but in different ways.

In general and simple terms, Fig. 4–12 shows how the two major types

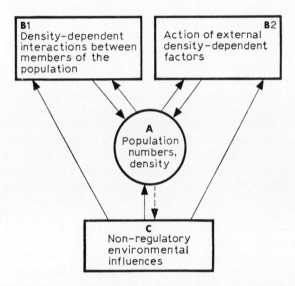

Fig. 4–12 Interactions of population density, density-dependent influences, and non-regulatory environmental influences. Further explanation in text.

of influence upon a population are related to population density and to each other. The arrows again run from the influent to the influenced items. Population density (A) is influenced by density-dependent interactions among the members of the population (B1), e.g. in interference or competition: these interactions are themselves influenced by the density of the population (hence the arrows pointing in opposite directions). Similarly, the action of external density-dependent factors (B2) upon the population is shown as being itself influenced by population density. For example, if a predator acts as a density-dependent factor, it is because it responds in a particular way to the level of population density of its prey. Last, but certainly not least, we have the general environmental factors whose influences (C) on the population are not significantly density-dependent; some of these influences may be weakly or inversely related to density (hence the dashed arrow), but they are predominantly density-independent. They include the action of factors like temperature and vegetation, which not only influence mortality and reproduction directly but also 'set the scene' for the population and largely determine how abundant it can be, by influencing the capacity of the habitat and the action of the regulatory density-dependent processes (hence the arrows from C to B1 and B2). These general environmental factors largely determine the conditions in the habitat, and so indirectly determine (a) which density-dependent factors are important in regulation at a particular time and place, and (b) which factors, density-dependent or otherwise, are the key factors, responsible for the main fluctuations in abundance from generation to generation.

Thus we may distinguish between the *regulation* of abundance (by one or more density-dependent processes) and the *determination* of abundance jointly by density-dependent processes and by general environmental factors which set the scene in the habitat and modify the action of the regulatory factors. Regulation may be brought about by a particular predator or by food shortage, for example, but the level of abundance at which this regulation tends to hold the population may vary greatly according to temperature, rainfall, the nature of the vegetation, or other factors.

We must look also to the whole complex, the life system, for a broad understanding of the nature of density-dependent processes. As we have remarked, many of these processes arise from competition within a population for resources in the habitat, e.g. food, refuges or space; the supply per individual depends on how many individuals there are, as well as on the total supply accessible in the habitat, and on the degree to which this may have been reduced by the population. If competitor species are present, they will join in this interaction between animals and resources, to the detriment of the first species. These relationships arise on the one hand from the limited carrying-capacity of the habitat with respect to the species concerned, and on the other hand from the competitive exploitation of the limited resources by this species.

Natural enemies cannot act upon a population as density-dependent (or delayed density-dependent) factors unless the severity of their attack responds in a particular way to the abundance of the population. Their response may be that of a population of animals competing in a density-dependent way for a food supply, the food being the population we are considering; or, as some birds do, they may concentrate on a prey species when (or where) it is abundant, but tend to ignore this species when (or where) it is sparse.

Density-dependence may be regarded as a relationship maintaining a stable equilibrium of numbers. If numbers rise above or fall below a particular equilibrium level, a density-dependent process geared to that level will intensify or relax, tending to steer the population back towards the equilibrium level. But it must be stipulated that, because of changes in the environment and often in the animals themselves, the equilibrium level tends to change continually, so that it would be difficult to identify it at any time: it is a stable but moving equilibrium.

In delayed density-dependence, the operative factor comes into action slowly or weakly at first, allowing some continuation of the rise of numbers above equilibrium level; then it overshoots the mark, forcing the numbers below the equilibrium level before relaxing. In this way it imposes oscillations on the population as well as regulating it.

Population Interactions 5

5.1 Types of interaction

The term 'population interactions' is applied to the influences upon each other of individuals or groups within a population, and also to the influences upon each other of populations of different species. There are other ways too in which different sorts of population interactions may be distinguished, and these various classifications cut across each other. For our present purpose, the first step is to decide what classifications seem relevant to population dynamics. Having done this, we may categorize a given interaction by recording its place in each of the significant classifications.

First, there is the above-mentioned distinction between interactions within a population (intraspecific) and those between different species (interspecific). Most of the examples mentioned in earlier chapters refer to intraspecific relationships, but relations between predator and prey, or herbivore and host plant, are interspecific.

Second, we may distinguish between favourable and unfavourable interactions. We do this on the assumption that abundance and high rates of survival and increase represent success and that an interaction promoting any of these is favourable, while an interaction reducing any of them is unfavourable. When grain mites first break into the germ of wheat grains, there is a co-operative interaction, for the pioneers make this food supply more accessible to the others. The result is favourable—a faster increase in numbers. In a culture of flour beetles, when the adults and larvae eat eggs and pupae, this cannibalistic predation is unfavourable, reducing the rates of survival and increase. The distinction between favourable and unfavourable is deliberately short-sighted. If we enquire whether it may be an advantage in the long run for the population to be hindered from becoming too abundant (and so perhaps from destroying its food supply), the answer may be both hard to discover and complicated.

Third, there is the difference between direct and indirect interactions. Predation is direct. But when animals damage the habitat by destroying shelter or food supply or by secreting toxins into it, the unfavourable effect upon their own or on a different population is indirect, *via* the environment.

Fourth, we may make a three-fold classification as follows. 'One-way' interactions are those in which A influences B, but A is not affected by B, as when, for example, large animals trample upon much smaller ones. Mutual interactions are those in which A and B influence each other in similar ways, e.g. by crowding, or by competing for food. If A and B influence each other in different ways, we need another adjective, such as 'disparate'. For example, if A is a predator and B is its prey, B is a favourable factor for A, while A is an unfavourable one for B.

Remembering the relationships discussed in Chap. 4, we might add another classification, distinguishing between density-related and density-independent interactions. It is hard to imagine population interactions that would not be affected in some degree by density, but the effects may be weak and difficult to demonstrate, in which case, for practical purposes, the interaction must be treated as density-independent. Density-related interactions might be subdivided into density-dependent and inverse, i.e. tending to regulate density or tending to steer it towards the higher or lower extremes.

From time to time the idea of 'competition' has been a subject of discussion among biologists interested in population interactions. They have used the word competition in the following ways:

(1) When numbers of the same or of different species make common use of a resource such as food, shelter or nesting sites, so that some individuals are hindered or deprived by the demands of the others, they are said to compete for the food etc.

(2) Members of the same or of different species may crowd, jostle or disturb each other, or even make lethal attacks (without being in the relation of true predators and prey). This may be regarded as something different from competition, but is sometimes treated as competition for space.

(3) Relationships such as those mentioned in (1) and (2) above may lead to the elimination from the area or habitat of one species by another. As in all cases of interspecific competition, the relative abundance of the two is important; hence their rates of reproduction and mortality, or of net increase, play a part in determining the outcome. Viewing the relationship as a whole, we may say the two species compete for the habitat, or for existence in the habitat. This may be appropriate even if neither is eliminated, and each survives in the parts where conditions give it the advantage. (It is commonly considered that the competition between species having similar requirements, especially food requirements, will be keener that that between species having different needs. 'Gause's hypothesis' argues from this that species with closely similar requirements cannot persist together in the same habitat. It also follows that competition should be most intense within a species, since many of its individuals have identical requirements.)

There have been differences of opinion whether 'competition' should include only (1), or (1) and (2), or all three of the above ideas. It may seem over-optimistic to expect to establish a precise technical meaning for a word which is used in the same sense and in others in common speech and writing. I shall not attempt the feat here, but shall use it like any other common word, hoping that, in its context, the meaning will be clear enough for the purpose in hand.

5.2 Forms of density-dependence

Recognizing the qualitative aspects of interactions is only a beginning. The investigator usually tries to describe them in quantitative terms. Special interest attaches to the form of the relationship between density and its effects. The investigator may hope that he will be able to analyse the more complex patterns into simple, elementary components, which he may be able to explain in biological terms.

The simplest relationship is one in which the effect of density is in direct proportion to density itself, as in Fig. 5-1 (main diagonal). If y stands for

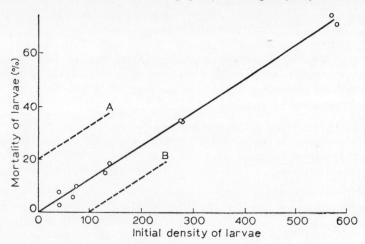

Fig. 5-1 Mortality of larvae of house flies in relation to initial numbers of larvae, in laboratory cultures. Lines A and B explained in text. (Data of BØGGILD, O. and KEIDING, J. (1958). *Oikos*, **9**, 1–25.)

proportional effect, d for density, and other letters represent constants, the relationship can be written $y = ad$. Lines such as A and B represent the relationships $y = ad + b$, and $y = a(d - c)$, which can also be written $y = ad - e$.

If a relationship appears as a curve on ordinary scales, it can sometimes be transformed to the more convenient straight line form in one way or another, e.g. by using logarithmic scales, as in Fig. 5-2b. The equation here is $\log y = \log a - b \log d$, or $y = ad^{-b}$ in Fig. 5-2a. If, instead of performance, we plot some adverse effect of density, and arrive at a straight line rising towards the right, the relationship is $\log y = \log a + b \log d$. On non-logarithmic scales the line curves upwards, and the corresponding equation is $y = ad^b$. This was used by Farr, in the 19th century, to express the relation between death-rate and density in human populations.

Density relationships often take on more complex forms than these, sometimes because of uncontrolled variables in the system, sometimes because they are combinations of two or more simpler relationships, some-

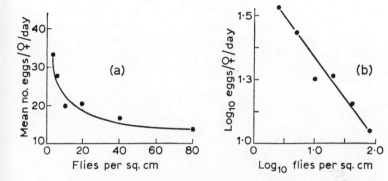

Fig. 5-2 Fecundity of fruit flies, *Drosophila melanogaster*, in relation to density of flies in a laboratory culture (a), and the same data on logarithmic scales (b). (Data of CHIANG, H. C., and HODSON, A. C. (1950). *Ecol. Monogr.*, **20**, 173–206.)

times, no doubt, because they are inherently different from the simple forms described above.

5.3   Interactions of predators and prey, or parasites and hosts

Predators are hunting animals which capture and kill their prey. Parasites are typically much smaller than their hosts and often do not kill them. Parasites include the microbes causing disease, i.e. pathogens. The relationships between populations of pathogens and those of man are dealt with in the science of epidemiology, which is the study of epidemics; in animal populations, outbreaks of microbial disease are called epizootics. Parasitic insects are sometimes called parasitoids, because they are often of the same order of size as their insect hosts, and usually kill them; but they are deposited on or within or near the host, usually as eggs, by the adult female parasite, so they are not predators.

A convenient starting point in the study of predator-prey interactions is to consider the factors influencing the rate of predation. One such factor is the abundance of the prey. If the prey is dense or numerous, a predator will be able to capture as many as it needs with a minimum of effort and time. If the prey is sparse, the predator will have to seek persistently even to catch only a few. As the prey density changes, so will the number taken by the predator. There is an underlying tendency for individual insect predators and parasitoids to take a fixed proportion of the available prey. If this tendency were fully realized, the graph of numbers taken against prey density would be a straight line, sloping upwards as density increased. However, the predators cannot in practice maintain such a response to a persistently rising density of prey; as they become satiated, predators will fail to respond to further increases in prey; moreover, they spend part of their time in 'handling' each captured prey, before they are ready to continue the hunt. Consequently, the potentially straight line turns over as density rises, becoming shallower in slope (Fig. 5–3). The Canadian biologist HOLLING (1959b) imitated this feature of insect predation, with a human 'predator'. Discs of sandpaper were scattered on a table, and the

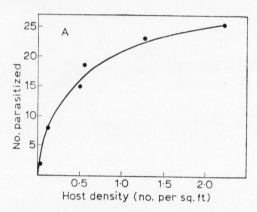

Fig. 5–3 Numbers (not percentage) of sawfly cocoons attacked by parasitic wasps searching for them under trees. (After HOLLING, 1959b, using data of BURNETT, 1958a.)

'predator', blindfolded, searched for them by touch. When the discs were numerous, the 'predator' spent more time in picking them up, and less in searching, so the percentage found in a given time was less. The result was a curve like that in Fig. 5–3.

HOLLING (1959a) also pointed out that vertebrate predators, such as mice and shrews hunting for the pupae of insects in ground litter, responded somewhat differently. When a particular species of prey was sparse, they took only a very low percentage, but at somewhat higher prey densities they took a higher percentage, developing a preference, a skill or a habit with respect to the hunting of this species. At much higher densities of prey the percentage captured fell away until the predator was taking a number that no longer increased with higher prey densities. This behaviour tends to produce a characteristic S-shaped curve as shown in Fig. 5–4.

These behaviour patterns of predators are named the 'functional response' (i.e. the response in the predation rate per individual predator to differences in prey density). Another possible reaction of predators to the density of their prey is to become more abundant by reproduction or aggregation when or where the prey is more numerous. Graphs of 'numerical responses' take various forms. The total response of a predator to prey density is of course the combined numerical and functional response. Total response is what normally concerns us first in a study of a predator-prey

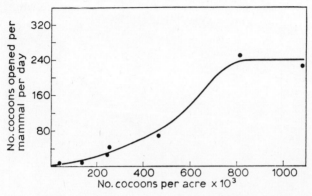

Fig. 5–4 Numbers (not percentage) of cocoons of pine sawfly discovered and destroyed in ground litter per day per individual predator (deer mouse, *Peromyscus*), in relation to the abundance of cocoons. (After HOLLING, 1959a.)

interaction; the analysis into numerical and functional components normally comes later. Holling has extended the analysis of predation by separating out the parts played by searching, pursuit, handling, digestive pauses, hunger, interference between predators, and so on, and constructing flow diagrams that can be a basis for computer programming. For each element, relationships can be formulated algebraically, studied experimentally, and thus given quantitative values appropriate to the situations studied.

Examination of the influence of prey density on the overall rate of predation was the first step in the analysis; it is the only step in this direction in many studies of predator-prey interactions. On the same level, another matter that has sometimes been investigated is the effect of the density of the predators themselves on the rate of predation. In experiments with insect parasitoids, the Canadian biologist BURNETT (1958b) found that the percentage parasitism was linearly proportional to the logarithm of parasite density (Fig. 5–5). The average number of parasite eggs per individual host was related in the same way to the log density of parasites. The fact that the rate of parasitism failed to increase in simple proportion to parasite density is a consequence of interference of some sort between the parasites (e.g. mutual repulsion, or avoidance of hosts already parasitized).

5.4 Competition and self-regulation among higher animals

Mammals and birds have relatively complex patterns of behaviour which are involved in competition for the resources of the habitat, and sometimes provide a regulation of abundance below the level that might be expected from the amount of these resources. Many mammals become more aggressive when their population density rises above a certain (variable) level, and

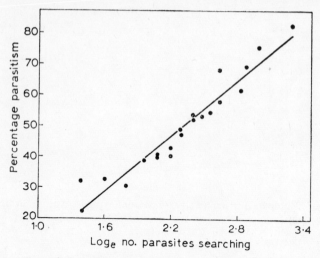

Fig. 5–5 Percentage of greenhouse whiteflies (*Trialeurodes*) parasitized by the hymenopteron *Encarsia*, in relation to the logarithm of parasite density, in experimental cultures undergoing the parasite-host oscillations. (After BURNETT, 1958b.)

this change is, sometimes at least, associated with a decline in the net rate of reproduction. In D. H. Chitty's studies of the field vole, populations seemed to undergo qualitative changes at high density, and these changes (notably an increased intra-specific aggressiveness and a reduced reproductive success) continued for some generations after the density had 'crashed' again to lower levels. These crashes occur about every fourth year in populations of the vole, as in those of some other rodents.

In many mammals serious fighting is largely avoided; but the animals carry out aggressive displays or 'token' fighting, in face of which one or other of the antagonists usually retreats before real damage is done. This substitution of ritual for real fighting is also common among birds, often associated with the defence of territories in the breeding season. In this way the habitat is divided among a number of breeding pairs, and when it is fully occupied the surplus individuals are forced to leave without breeding. Birds in flocks also compete among themselves for food in the winter, and again serious fighting tends to be avoided: each bird gives way to certain others, but is given precedence by the remainder. Those near the bottom of the 'peck-order' are the first to die when food is in short supply.

In such ways the resources of the habitat are efficiently exploited; if these resources were more equally divided among too many animals, few of the animals might rear their young successfully or (in the winter) survive food shortage. These behaviour patterns tend to ensure that the successful competitors get enough for their needs, and that relatively little of the resources are wasted on individuals that are going to fail. To use the terms suggested by A. J. Nicholson, 'scramble' is replaced by 'contest'.

The advantages to the species of this arrangement are as obvious as the advantages of avoiding serious fighting, in which even the victors might be injured. On the basis of these and other considerations, WYNNE-EDWARDS (1962) considers that many animals have evolved ritual social displays which serve to provide an assessment of the size of the population and of the surplus that must be excluded. Many of his arguments, and those of Andrewartha and Birch against the theory of density-dependent regulation, are discussed critically by LACK (1966, Appendix).

Plant Population Dynamics

6.1 Similarities and differences between plant and animal populations

For the purposes of population dynamics, plants differ from animals in some respects, and resemble them in others. If we choose particular features for the comparison (e.g. reproduction, competition) we often find both resemblances and differences.

Like those of animals, populations of any one species of plant are found in particular types of habitat. Plants tend to be specially dependent on certain soil characteristics (acidity, water regime etc.), whereas many animals are dependent primarily on the presence of a particular type of vegetation, and some require one particular species of plant.

Individual plants mature, reproduce and die. Plants, like animals, include ephemeral and long-lived species and, like animals, often produce large numbers of potential young, most of which never become established. Many plants reproduce or extend themselves vegetatively, by means of bulbils, runners, rhizomes etc., giving rise to mats of vegetation in which it is difficult to decide where individuals begin and end. But aggregation of most plants arises largely because of their immobility as individuals, in contrast to most animals, which are free to disperse. The fixity of plants makes some sorts of population study easier than with animals which are frequently on the move.

Like animals, plants compete for food materials and for space; in general, they compete more for light and moisture than animals do. Plants are in general more variable in size, according to the environmental conditions and the intensity of competition.

Plant populations, like those of animals, wax and wane as conditions change, but often more slowly. Like animals, they are restricted in number or in biomass by the limited supply of things they require, such as food, space, access to light etc. (hence the competition for these requisites). Like animals, they may be limited by the attacks of natural enemies—herbivores, and possibly some pathogenic micro-organisms.

Like populations of animals, those of plants are made up of individuals differing in genetic constitution, except in clones (a clone is a group descended from an individual parent by asexual reproduction); these are commoner in plant than in animal populations. Genetic differences between individuals are the raw material of evolution by natural selection. This process is generally envisaged as influencing the genetic pattern of a species over a wide area and on a time-scale reckoned in thousands of years. But there is evidence, in both plants and animals, of much more rapid, though smaller, genetic changes, particularly in response to the conditions of a newly invaded or a newly changed habitat. Some investigators claim that rapid changes in the genetic pattern of a population may, to some extent, reflect changes in its density, and so may enter into the dynamics of its regulation.

6.2   Density effects and competition among plants

To say that plants compete for resources is to imply the existence of density effects comparable to those among animals. Such effects have been demonstrated and measured experimentally. As among animals, different density effects vary in form when graphed and have been interpreted by means of various algebraic equations. Two examples will suffice to show their similarity in principle to the corresponding relationships of animals.

In Canberra, Australia, DONALD (1961) set up experiments with clover on small field plots, to compare the effects of different plant densities upon yield (the crop of plant material that could be harvested). He supplied ample water and nutrients to the plots, so there was no competition until the plants grew large enough to compete with each other for light. In Fig. 6–1a, the lowest line represents the early, non-competitive stage, in which

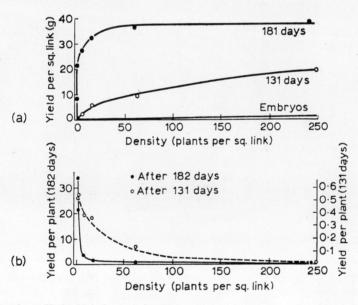

Fig. 6–1   Yield (dried crop) from clover plants at various densities, competing for light in experimental plots; (a) yield per unit area, (b) yield per plant. ((a) After DONALD, 1961; courtesy of Cambridge Univ. Press. (b) Based on same data.)

the yield per unit area was directly proportional to the number of plants involved. The two upper lines show how, as time passed and the plants grew larger and began to cast shade upon each other, the yield per unit area in the denser plots (on the right in the graph) became less and less dependent on the number of plants there, and after 181 days had approached a constant maximal value. The total amount of the crop was finally determined by the supply of sunlight; if one plot had more plants than another, then these more numerous plants were smaller. In Fig. 6–1b, these results are converted to a form comparable with that of Fig. 5–2a.

The second example concerns experiments in which PALMBLAD (1968) reared single-species populations of plants in pots. He started with 1, 5, 50,

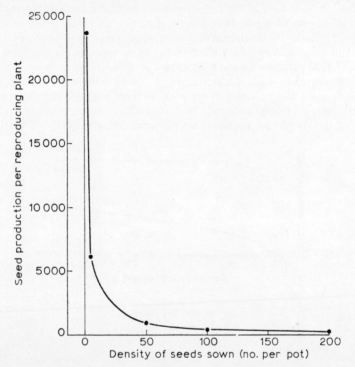

Fig. 6–2   Results of experiments with shepherd's purse (*Capsella*) in plant pots. Data of PALMBLAD (1968).

100 and 200 seeds per pot, and observed the plants which grew from them. Among other things, he recorded the number of seeds formed per plant which achieved the reproductive phase. When his observed values are graphed against the initial density of seeds per pot (Fig. 6–2), the points follow a curve analogous to those of Fig. 6–1b.

The above are instances of density effects associated with intraspecific competition. Interspecific competition also occurs among plants: this has been inferred both from field observations and from experiments. What happens may depend a good deal on whether the different species begin growth at the same time, or one is already established when another begins. When a crop is sown, crop and weeds may begin growth together. Such a situation was studied experimentally by ASPINALL and MILTHORPE (1959), using spring barley and white persicaria (*Polygonum lapathifolium*) emerging on the same day in pots. Fig. 6–3 shows the growth in dry weight

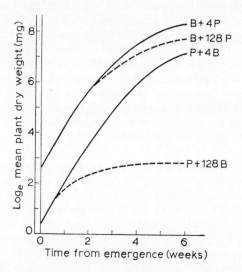

Fig. 6–3   Relationship with time of the logarithms of dry weight per plant of barley (B) surrounded by 4 or 128 white persicaria plants (P), and of persicaria surrounded by 4 or 128 barley plants. (After MILTHORPE, 1961; courtesy of Cambridge Univ. Press.)

of barley surrounded by four persicaria, and of persicaria surrounded by four barley (not enough for significant competition), compared with the growth of each species when surrounded by 128 of the other. The curves show that the effect of persicaria on barley was relatively slight, whereas the effect of barley on persicaria was great. This result arose from the fact that the persicaria at emergence was much smaller than the barley, and could not overcome this initial disadvantage.

As with animals, the influence of plants upon each other is not necessarily adverse. Apart from some being dependent on others parasitically or for support, some do better in the presence of other species than in a single-species stand. For example, HARPER (1960) found that when he sowed seeds of poppy (*Papaver*) with wheat, under some conditions more poppy plants were produced than when poppy was sown alone: it seemed that the presence of the wheat plants increased the number of sites suitable for the development of poppy plants.

It is often found that competition is more severe between members of the same species than between members of different species. In stands of poppies, HARPER and MCNAUGHTON (1962) showed that the chances of establishment of a particular species from seed were higher in the presence of other species of poppy than in pure culture, for a given total density. WHITTINGTON and O'BRIEN (1968) found that mixed species of grasses gave a higher yield than did one species alone. We may interpret this as meaning that plants of the same species competed more intensely than did those of different species, because their requirements were more similar (cf. p. 33).

The ultimate outcome of competition between two species may be the displacement of one of them from the habitat. Field observations continued over a long enough period often show some species becoming more abundant while others become sparser. Sometimes a population of one species may be seen to advance upon and displace that of another species: WATT (1955) observed a continuous front of bracken invading and gradually replacing a stand of heather (rabbit grazing may have been a complicating factor).

Competitive displacement may also be demonstrated experimentally. SAGAR and HARPER (1961) removed grasses with a selective herbicide in patches of various grassland habitats near Oxford, to test the effect of this upon plantains (*Plantago*). They also sowed seeds of plantain in existing grassland. The results suggested that in some of the communities the grasses had an important influence on the presence or absence of particular species of plantains (as well as on their abundance when present). In the laboratory, CLATWORTHY and HARPER (1962) demonstrated the exclusion of one species of duckweed (*Lemna*) by another. They found, incidentally, that the winner in such a contest between species was not necessarily the one that was denser in pure cultures. (The same has been observed in experiments with different species of flour beetles: cf. PARK (1955, 1962).)

6.3   Regulation of plant populations

In relatively simple situations such as in laboratory cultures, it is obvious that the limited supply of space or of nutrients sets a limit to the number of individuals that can exist there, even allowing for the often stunted size of crowded individuals. Well-developed density effects, such as those referred to in §6.2, can exert regulation if other factors allow the population to reach the levels of abundance at which they operate.

Among the natural enemies of plants, certain herbivores at least are known to act as regulatory agents. A clear witness to this is the success achieved in the economic control of certain weeds by the introduction of appropriate insects. A classic example of such biological control is the introduction of the moth *Cactoblastis* to eastern Australia to deal with prickly pear, a group of cacti comprising several species of *Opuntia* (Plate 2). These introduced plants had by 1925 taken over some 30 million acres of country with their thickets of spiny lobes. When *Cactoblastis* became established, its caterpillars rapidly destroyed the major pest cacti, and it increased and spread to surrounding areas. The economic problem was thus effectively solved by the late 1930's. But the insects did not completely eradicate the prickly pear. There were usually plants which escaped attack and continued growing; the stands developing from these were usually found at a later date by egg-laying *Cactoblastis* moths, and were decimated by the caterpillars before reaching any considerable size. (From many areas the survivors of insect attack were removed by cultivation.)

Another well-known example is the control of St. John's wort, *Hypericum perforatum*, by means of leaf-beetles of the genus *Chrysolina*. This weed is a pest of grazing land in many parts of the world, displacing useful forage, and poisoning stock when eaten in quantity. In California the beetles have exerted a spectacular degree of control, reducing St. John's wort to about a hundredth of its former abundance. They have been successful too in some parts of Australia, though not in others. In many of the areas where the weed persists, the beetles keep it at a much reduced level of abundance.

For our present purpose, the point of these examples is the evidence they provide of the great impact that insects can make upon the abundance of plants. In many studies of plant populations the possible influence of insects has been neglected.

Larger herbivores should also be considered. When the appearance and spread of myxomatosis in Britain in the 1950s removed the rabbits from many parts of the country, some of the consequent changes in the vegetation were obvious to anyone who knew the areas concerned, and many less obvious changes were recorded by plant ecologists. Some grasses and woody plants increased in size and abundance, and other species lost ground in competition with these. There was a noticeable decline of ragwort (*Senecio jacobaea*); and in many places where rabbits have re-established themselves the ragwort has again become a prominent feature (and sometimes a danger to stock).

A method of demonstrating the influence of grazing on vegetation is to set up enclosures. Where grazers such as rabbits or sheep are important, their exclusion from plots produces a rapid and striking increase in the amount of vegetation, with changes too in the relative abundance of different species.

Economic and Social Population Problems

7.1 Crops as populations

Cereals, vegetables, fruits and other useful crops are mostly grown in monoculture, i.e. as plant populations of a single species. By dint of cultivation, use of fertilizers and judicious spacing, the grower aims to reap the maximum harvest per acre of land, and to maintain a high level of quality. As standards rise, commonsense and experience need more and more to be reinforced by research, including research into the relations of the plants to one another, as members of a population. Obviously too sparse a crop will waste land and encourage weeds. But too dense a sowing or planting will also waste material, and give rise to unfavourable density effects and wasteful competition (§6.2). One of the aims of the plant breeder is to develop varieties that will tolerate high densities with the minimum of harmful competition. One of the functions of research is to clothe these bare principles with quantitative information, applying to particular crops, soils, climates and methods.

At the same time, since competition tends to be most intense between organisms with the same requirements, there are advantages in growing different crops together. (There are other advantages too: one crop may protect a second, or a leguminous crop may raise the supply of available nitrogen for another.) Sometimes these benefits more than offset the advantages of monoculture, which is simpler to manage and more amenable to mechanical husbandry.

7.2 Populations of pests

Any animal that damages crops or domestic animals or disturbs our own comfort or health may be called a pest. But, economically, there is a vast difference between a major pest and one that is rare or incidental. This difference is chiefly a matter of abundance. With a few exceptions, a major pest is one that is abundant, or that can become so at times and in certain circumstances.

Many pest populations are notably unstable: periods of low density are interrupted by occasional and sometimes sudden increases ('outbreaks'; cf. Fig. 4–2). A pre-requisite for this sort of population pattern is a high rate of increase under favourable conditions. As we have seen, this may be achieved either by the production of numerous eggs or young by each female, or by a rapid passage through several generations, or, of course, both.

The reasons why some species are abundant or common in a particular region while others are sparse or rare is generally unknown. In principle, it is clear that various characteristics of a species and of its environment may be important in determining its abundance, e.g. (1) its requirements of food, physical conditions, cover, breeding sites etc., and the extent to which the environment fulfils these requirements, (2) its reproductive capacity under favourable conditions, and (3) the presence and abundance of various natural enemies, competitors and pathogens. For a few animals that have been intensively studied it is possible to specify which factors chiefly determine their abundance, but for most species this remains to be discovered.

Many species which reach high densities as pests of cultivation do not seem to be abundant in their natural environments. Natural communities tend to be complex, with a varied flora and fauna. Whether in virtue simply of this complexity, or because in addition natural communities have evolved a self-adjusting balance, it seems that any tendency for particular species of animals to be very abundant is commonly offset by a series of opposing influences. It has been claimed that predators and parasites are limited by the availability of prey, while herbivores are limited by the attacks of such natural enemies. If this were accepted without qualifications, we should have to explain the success of biological control of weeds as being made possible only by introducing herbivorous insects without their natural enemies. Be that as it may, there is no doubt that many species reach much higher levels of abundance on crops than they do under natural conditions. In contrast to the stabilizing complexity of nature, monoculture provides a simplified or impoverished set of conditions, with relatively few of the controlling mechanisms that operate in nature. Moreover, the environment of monoculture is relatively uniform; if it is favourable to a pest, it is likely to be widely favourable, whereas in nature the habitat is much more varied, and is unlikely to be favourable everywhere at once. Again, the use of insecticides to control the pests often kills most of their natural enemies, so that there are few natural controls to rely on if the chemicals should fail (and they often do fail, after a time, through the development of insecticide resistance in the pests). In managed forest, the recurrence of severe outbreaks of pests in single-species stands has led to the adoption of a policy of mixed-species woodlands in many areas.

The way in which the above general points apply to particular pests must of course be discovered by research. When this is done, the results often suggest ways of improving the control of the pest. For example, the bullfinch is a pest of orchards in Britain, stripping off the buds of trees and bushes in the latter part of the winter. Since these birds do not move far from their home ground, their numbers can be usefully reduced by trapping in and about the orchards. The natural tendency has been to set the traps at the time when the damage is being done. Now research by NEWTON (1967) at Oxford has confirmed that the bullfinch feeds on the

seeds of various plants such as nettles and docks in the early winter, and
that when these supplies are exhausted they move on to ash seeds. The
crop of ash seeds varies greatly from year to year; on roughly alternate
years there is a very poor crop. It is in these winters that the bullfinch, run-
ning short of seeds, turns to buds as a major item of food, preferring the
buds of the cultivated fruit plants to those of wild trees and shrubs.
Newton points out that if orchardists are to rely on reducing the numbers of
bullfinches by trapping, they should catch them at the beginning of winter,
before they have depleted the stock of weed seeds. Then the survivors will
be less dependent on the ash seeds, less likely to exhaust them, and so less
likely to turn to the orchards in late winter.

7.3   Biological control of pests

The biological control of pests, by the introduction and establishment of
parasites, predators or pathogens, has been more often used than has the
biological control of weeds, described in §6.3. One of the most successful
and best-known examples is the control of the cottony-cushion scale,
Icerya purchasi, in California by the introduction of the predatory ladybird
beetle *Rodolia cardinalis* in the late nineteenth century (Plate 1). Scale insects are related to the aphids, and suck the sap from plants. *Icerya* is a pest
of citrus trees; a heavy infestation can severely damage the shoots, even
killing the trees at times. It forms a conspicuous white waxy bag in which
numerous eggs are laid. It is native to Australia, from which it was acci-
dentally introduced on young trees to California. There it flourished
remarkably, and became a serious threat to orange groves. The entomolo-
gist A. Koebele travelled to Australia to seek its natural enemies, and sent
back the *Rodolia* ladybird. Where this was released in California it rapidly
reduced the populations of *Icerya* to such a low level that it was often hard
to find any. Outbreaks of the scale occurred from time to time in places
that the ladybird had not reached, or where it had been killed by insecticides; but the introduction of the ladybird to the infested orchards has
demonstrated again and again its ability to bring about rapid and entirely
satisfactory control of the pest. In its native Australia the scale is usually
not abundant, and there is no doubt that *Rodolia* and other natural enemies
are at least partly responsible for its low numbers. When it was taken to
California without its natural enemies, it multiplied alarmingly, and was
regulated only at a very high density at the limits of its food supply. When
the ladybird was introduced *Icerya* was reduced to very low numbers, and
generally held there, its abundance regulated at a much lower level by this
predator.

An interesting short account of some recent examples of biological control
is given by WATERHOUSE and WILSON (1968). For a comprehensive treatment the volume edited by DEBACH (1964) may be consulted. Many of the
big successes in biological control have been with species of pests or of weeds

Plate 1

(*above*)   A small swarm of desert locusts (*Schistocerca gregaria*) photographed from the air in Kenya in 1953. Swarm moving towards left,
and covering about 1 sq. km. (Photographed by J. Sayer, reproduced
by courtesy of Anti-Locust Research Centre, London.)

(*below*)   The cottony-cushion scale (*Icerya purchasi*) and a predatory
ladybird *Rodolia koebelei*. The related *R. cardinalis* is the species which
mainly controls the scale. (Courtesy Mr. F. Wilson, Sirex Biological
Control Unit, Ascot, Berks.)

Plate 2 A stand of prickly pear (*Opuntia*) before and after attack by caterpillars of *Cactoblastis* (*centre*). (Reproduced by courtesy of Survey Branch, Lands Department, Queensland and C.S.I.R.O., Canberra, Australia.)

that, like *Icerya*, were introduced to new regions without their natural enemies. The introduction of suitable parasites, predators or herbivores has restored the missing regulatory factors which keeps their numbers at a low level in their native environment.

In Britain, most pests are native to the region, and this is probably one reason why relatively few attempts at biological control have been made. The minute parasitic wasp *Aphelinus mali* was introduced in the 1920s to control the woolly aphis of apple trees, but for climatic or other reasons it was not the success that it was in various warmer countries. In heated greenhouses, useful control of the whitefly *Trialeurodes vaporariorum* (related to scales and aphids) has sometimes been achieved by the introduction of another minute parasitic wasp. The younger stages of the greenhouse whitefly are scale-like, but the adult is a delicate winged insect dusted over with a white waxy powder. The scales and adults of the whitefly suck the sap of plants such as cucumbers and tomatoes. There is a tendency for its populations and those of the parasite to generate parasite-host oscillations, which are a nuisance for practical control and an object of study for some experimentalists.

Besides insect parasites and predators, pathogenic bacteria and viruses have occasionally been used with success in the control of insect pests (DeBACH, 1964). For example, the European pine and spruce sawflies have been successfully controlled in parts of Canada by introduction of appropriate viruses. As a class, viruses have the virtue of being highly specific, so that no danger to beneficial insects is involved. The bacterium *Bacillus thuringiensis* has been used with some success against various caterpillars (NORRIS, 1965). Attempts at biological control with fungi have been made, but with limited success, perhaps chiefly because they remain effective only under moist conditions.

In recent years a number of new types of biological control have been tried, and used successfully in a few instances. One method is to release large numbers of adults of the pest species made reproductively sterile by exposure to a radioactive source or to a chemical sterilant; if enough of the normal population mate with the sterile individuals instead of with each other, the reproductive rate will fall below that necessary to maintain the population, and the numbers will decline with increasing rapidity to zero.

7.4   The impact of modern insecticides

The control of pests by means of toxic chemicals, applied as sprays, dusts or as gases, has been practised for over a century. Some of these measures were quite successful in reducing damage by the pests to acceptable levels, but many pests were not adequately controlled.

The introduction in the years since 1940 of a series of very successful new insecticides, beginning with DDT, marked a new era in the history of pest control. For a time, it seemed to many people that biological methods of control could be discarded. However, serious weaknesses in the strategy of control by insecticides gradually claimed the attention of economic entomologists. The killing of natural enemies enabled insects and mites that had been obscure minor pests to become a major problem. For example, the use of DDT in orchards to control codling moth and other pests led to severe outbreaks of fruit tree red spider mite.

Another difficulty attending the intensive use of insecticides is one already mentioned—the appearance of resistant strains of pests. All species exhibit inheritable individual variations, and there is often a minute fraction of an insect or mite population which carries genes conferring a relatively high resistance to the pesticide employed. If these few individuals survive a treatment, the population derived from them will be more resistant than the original one. If the same insecticide is used repeatedly, the process of selection will continue and the population will become increasingly resistant. Such an increase of resistance may be both rapid and striking: strains that, by certain criteria, are hundreds or even thousands of times as resistant as the original population may be developed. The nature of this resistance has been intensively studied by biochemists and geneticists. Biochemically, it has been shown in some cases to involve breakdown of the insecticide by the insect's metabolic processes. Genetically, it has been shown to be inherited in some instances as a simple Mendelian unit factor, in others by a more complex genetic pattern. Occasionally the factor selected has proved to be a behaviour pattern which enables the pest to escape fatal contact with the insecticide. Physiological resistance to one insecticide confers resistance also to others that are chemically related to it; hence, although it is often possible to deal with the situation by changing to a different type of insecticide, there are relatively few groups at present available which differ sufficiently from each other for this purpose; there is therefore a danger that, as resistance is developed to several categories of chemicals in turn, some pests may exhaust the available armoury of insecticides.

7.5   Integrated control and pest management

Largely as a result of the above difficulties associated with complete reliance on insecticides, many economic biologists have adopted, or returned to, a more comprehensive strategy of pest control. A first step in this direction is the idea of 'integrated control'—the use of insecticides in conjunction with biological control. In one form, this means the use of insecticides that are more selective than the earlier 'broad spectrum' ones such as DDT, so as to control the pest but allow the survival of a sufficient number of natural enemies to continue its control for some time afterwards. The seasonal timing of the insecticide treatment can also be chosen so as to cause minimal damage to useful predators or parasites. Timing has always been a consideration for other reasons—to avoid killing bees and other pollinating insects, and to avoid poisoning the final product; hence sprays are normally not applied at the flowering time in orchards, nor on fruit or vegetables near harvest time. Another way of ensuring the survival of some natural enemies is to leave certain patches untreated, a policy that is justified if one has reason to think that the enemies will more than compensate for the pests that are spared with them.

A second type of integrated control is to apply chemical and artificial (as distinct from natural) biological control in combination. A plan of this sort was proposed by the British entomologists HUSSEY, PARR and GOULD (1965) for the control of the mite *Tetranychus urticae* infesting cucumbers in glasshouses. The introduced predatory mite *Phytoseiulus riegeli* has been shown to give good temporary control of *Tetranychus*. The plan was to introduce numbers of the predator (e.g. about 10 per plant) on two successive occasions about two months apart, and later to apply chemicals to protect the plants in the later stages of their life.

A more comprehensive view of integrated control underlies the idea of 'pest management' (CLARK *et al.*, 1967). This idea is in line with the views of many ecologists; it seeks to take due account of all significant elements in the pest-crop-environment situation, not only selective insecticides and natural enemies, but also methods of husbandry, the possibility of developing varieties having a greater inherent resistance to attack, and any other factor which it may be possible to modify advantageously. In such an approach, the ecology of the pest, and especially its population dynamics, calls for special attention.

The mere adoption of this comprehensive viewpoint does not of course automatically provide a means of modifying the situation so as to control the pest. For any particular species, expensive and time-consuming research is required to fill out this broad picture with factual information. Meanwhile, attempts to find a quick solution, or at least a helpful palliative, must be continued. But perhaps they will be increasingly planned with an eye to their making contributions towards a comprehensive understanding of the situation.

7.6   Man as a predator

It is only relatively recently in the history of man, in the Neolithic cultural stage, that the gathering of plant food and the hunting of animals ceased to be the basic activity of most human communities, and were superseded by agriculture and the domestication of animals. These earlier ways of life have of course not disappeared, and indeed some forms of hunting—e.g. that of fish and whales from the sea—have greatly increased in modern times. Primitive man probably lacked the skills and numbers to endanger the survival of the species he preyed upon. Today man is very differently placed in this respect. Modern vessels and techniques have enabled him to reduce the abundance of some marine fish to a level at which further fishing is in danger of becoming an uneconomic activity; for lack of international agreement, the whaling industry appears to be foundering, and the blue whale of the southern seas has been so reduced that the survival of the species is in doubt. Wanton shooting and slaughter led to the extinction of the passenger pigeon and the near-extinction of the bison in North America.

Although the ethical, social and political aspects of these matters are a legitimate concern of biologists, here we must concentrate on the problems of population dynamics which are involved. If a predator becomes so efficient that its prey cannot maintain itself, the predator must subsist on other food, or else die out itself. Man should use his wits and his social organization to ensure that he does not continue to endanger the survival of valuable prey species. He must study the population dynamics of his prey, and estimate realistically the degree of exploitation it can stand without loss of yield.

British marine biologists have been concerned with the effects of overfishing by our own and other European fleets in the seas around our coasts and northwards to Iceland. The cessation of fishing during the two world wars led to great increases in the stocks of fish in these seas, by over 100 per cent in some areas. The late E. S. Russell summarized the dynamics of these populations in the equation

$$S_2 = S_1 (A+G)-(C+M),$$

where S_2 is the weight of fish large enough to be retained by the meshes of the particular nets used in the fishery, at the end of the year; S_1 is the corresponding weight at the beginning of the year; A represents the addition to the stock provided by young fish growing up to a catchable size; G is the addition provided by the growth of fish beyond the minimum catchable size; C is the weight of fish caught during the year; and M is the weight lost by natural death of some of the fish that are not caught. The equation is simply a convenient list of the gains and losses that must be estimated and set against each other as factors influencing the exploitable fish population. A few numerical examples of the influence of different rates of fishing on the population, and references to the main works on this subject, are given by HARDY (1959; see also PHILLIPSON, 1966, pp. 51–3).

7.7   Populations of domesticated animals

Although the transition from hunting to the domestication of animals may have begun 10,000 or more years ago, it is still going on. More species are being domesticated and the numbers of individuals reared are continually increasing. There is also an intermediate stage, the culling of herds that are wild but 'managed' as regards their abundance and range of wandering. Fully domesticated animals have been spread widely through the world but have not always done well. It has been suggested that the management of some of the wild herbivores in parts of Africa might be the most economic way of exploiting the land for man's benefit. On the island of Rhum, off the west coast of Scotland, wild red deer have been found to give a better yield than sheep did there.

Stock-raisers whose animals are free-ranging are concerned with the carrying capacity of the land—the number of grazing sheep or cattle per acre that it will maintain permanently. With more intensive methods the animals are maintained at an artificially high density in fenced areas, moved periodically from a grazed area to a rested one, and provided with supplementary feed in various forms.

In free-range or in natural conditions, the relationship of grazing animals to the vegetation of their pastures is similar to that of predators and prey in one respect—that the ultimate limits to the abundance of the grazers are set by their food supply. This form of limitation may seldom operate under truly natural conditions, where predators tend to keep the density of grazers at a much lower level than their food supply would do. But when these natural controlling agents are eliminated, the food supply will be the limiting factor unless human predation—planned culling of the herds—is applied so as to keep the numbers down to a reasonable level. This has not always been done, and in many regions sheep, goats or cattle have been allowed to overtax and degrade the land.

The rate of increase of animals is another major concern of the grazer and stockbreeder. A high rate of reproduction provides a large annual surplus that can be killed or marketed. The rate of increase of different species of farm animals varies enormously. In her first 3 years a cow normally produces one calf. But a sow will produce her first litter at 9 months, and thereafter have two litters per year, with an average of 8 young in each; so in the first 3 years, if all her descendants were kept and allowed to breed, their total would be 2,220 (HAMMOND, 1955).

7.8 Human populations

In earlier sections of this book we noticed the following aspects of the dynamics of animal populations. (1) Numbers tend to increase up to the capacity of the environment, i.e. up to the limit of supply of some essential resource, often food. (2) But the capacity of the environment may undergo frequent fluctuations, and sometimes a permanent change, due to changes in weather or climate, or because of changes in the vegetation or the effects of various animals. The response of a population to such changes cannot usually occur all at once; part at least of it requires time to develop, especially when the response is a reproductive increase. Moreover, numbers in a population are often held below the level they could otherwise reach, as a result of (3) the competition of other species that take a part of the limiting resources, (4) interference or predation among its own members, or (5) the attacks of predators, parasites or pathogens. Some or all of these processes may operate in combination.

In human populations all of these phenomena have been evident at various times and places. (1) Hunger, malnutrition and recurrent famines in certain regions have testified to man's tendency to increase to the limits of the current resources of the local environment, although other factors have often been involved, e.g. migration, the adverse effects of disease on productive efficiency, also (2) effects of adverse weather on crops, and damage to the environment by over-exploitation and misuse. (3) Our food supply is reduced by the activities of competitor species—pests that attack livestock, growing crops and stored food. (4) Warfare, ritual sacrifice and infanticide represent human versions of interference and predation within the species. (5) Predators of man are scarcely a significant factor nowadays, but in some regions diseases such as malaria (due to parasites transmitted by mosquitoes), sleeping sickness (due to parasites transmitted by tsetse flies in Africa) and infectious diseases like smallpox (caused by a virus) still have an important influence on man's abundance.

In spite of the various processes opposing its growth, the human population has increased slowly through the ages. Since the seventeenth century, with rapid technical advances in control over the environment and the causes of disease, the rate of increase has continuously accelerated. The world population is roughly estimated to have been 906 million in 1800, 1,171 million in 1850, 1,608 million in 1900, and 2,407 million in 1950. Not only have our numbers continued to grow, but the proportional rate of increase has been rising: the above estimates represent increases of 29 per cent, 38 per cent and 50 per cent in these three equal periods. This acceleration is still evident, for the estimated population in 1968 was 3,300 million. By studying recent trends, demographers have made extrapolations into the future. One such projection suggests a total of about 5,000 million in 1985, and another suggests about 6,000 million in the year 2000.

The above figures for the total population of past years are inaccurate, because they are based partly on unreliable and incomplete censuses in many parts of the world. But the more complete and reliable figures from the advanced countries confirm the general trend, and there is little basis at present for any expectation that the rate of world population increase is about to decline.

An increase in abundance can come about by way of a rise in percentage reproductive rate, while the percentage death rate remains steady, or by way of a decline in the death rate while the reproductive rate remains unchanged; or both may increase, or both decrease, so long as the reproductive rate increases more, or declines less, than the death rate does. Data for human populations of various countries show that birth rates and death rates have both been declining (Table 4). The death rate, i.e. yearly deaths per 1000 of population, is a faulty index of mortality since it takes no account of the age composition of the population or of the incidence of

Table 4   Birth rates and death rates per 1000 of population in several countries: Great Britain, from article on Population by D. V. Glass in *Chambers's Encyclopaedia* (1959 edition); India and Japan, from RUSSELL (1954).

Years	1861–5	1901–5	1921–5	1940	1941–5	1946–50	1948	1950
Great Britain								
Births	35·1	28·3	20·3		16·1	18·2		
Deaths	22·5	16·2	12·3		12·9	11·9		
India								
Births				31·4			25·4	
Deaths				20·7			16·0	
Japan								
Births				29·5				28·3
Deaths				16·5				10·9

deaths in different age-groups. Because of this, demographers prefer to construct a life table and derive from it the mean expectation of life at birth. This index shows a steady increase, for example from 44·6 years for females in England and Wales in 1871–80 to 71·5 years in 1950–52, confirming the trend suggested by the cruder death rate figures. It seems, then, that birth rates have been declining, but death rates have been declining more. The reduction in death rates is attributable to the improvement in the living standards and hygiene in many parts of the world, and to the even more widespread application of modern advances in medicine and in the control of malaria-carrying mosquitoes, for example, by means of modern insecticides. The overall rate of increase would have been greater than it has been but for the effects of wars and famines and the epidemics that have tended to follow in their train. There is, however, another and very potent factor operating to reduce the birth rate. This is the widespread preference for small families by people who have had the benefits of at least a moderately good standard of living and education, and who are no longer faced with the probability of a high mortality among their children.

We have seen that, although there has been an overall decline in birth rate, the fall in death rate has been faster, and that consequently the population is increasing more and more rapidly. This is specially so in the poorer countries, where the resultant hardship is greatest and the food supply already insufficient. It is the relation of numbers to food supply that gives the greatest cause for anxiety. There is a race between increasing population and increasing food supply, the latter brought about by improving methods of production and the fuller exploitation of some sources such as fisheries. Overall, the food producers are slowly gaining, but the benefits are unevenly distributed. In Latin America and Africa, food and population were increasing at about the same rate until droughts caused a poor harvest in 1965–6 and brought a reduction of 4 to 5 per cent in the food available per person. In many countries supplies are so near subsistence level that droughts and wars soon bring starvation in their wake. Just as some countries are well supplied and have more problems of over-eating than of malnutrition, while others live precariously near the mini-mum for subsistence, so in these poorer countries some sections of the community are well fed while others go hungry. Countries which produce a surplus of food could often produce more still, but difficulties of economics and transport have to be overcome in order to make the effort worth-while to the growers and get the surplus to all the places where it is needed. Since these problems cannot easily be solved, it is important that in each region the population should remain within the limits set by that region's current ability to produce or import an adequate food supply. Improve-ments in food production must be continued as quickly as possible, especi-ally in the regions most in need. Efforts are being made, and should be extended, to persuade people of the wisdom and necessity of limiting the size of families.

If such efforts should fail, and the population were to increase appreci-ably more than the food supply, the result would inevitably be disastrous. Assuming, more optimistically, that the supply of food will in future grow somewhat faster than the population does, there must still be limits be-yond which population density cannot go. Simple lack of space would be the ultimate limit, but psychological factors would intervene at a much lower density. It is to be hoped that rational planning of our abundance will be achieved in time to avert a global population disaster.

In a population that is neither increasing nor decreasing, the birth rate and death rate are of course equal. At present the death rate in the more advanced countries seems to be moving towards a value of about 10 per 1000 per year. For stability, the birth rate would have to be reduced to the same level.

This brief discussion has perhaps shown that the simple principles of population dynamics apply to human populations, but that economic, social and psychological factors also play an important part, just as organ-ized behaviour patterns do among the social animals. The population dynamics of a species can be understood only in relation to its way of life, its behaviour, its environment, the way it goes about getting food and other necessities, and, in the case of man, in relation to the way he feels and thinks.

Exercises

Directions for a number of convenient practical exercises in population dynamics are given by ANDREWARTHA (1961), LEWIS and TAYLOR (1967) and in the volume edited by LAMBERT (1967). MACARTHUR and CONNELL (1966) describe several relevant laboratory exercises.

The following are a few exercises for calculation. Like those in the text of some earlier sections, some are much simplified versions of more realistic problems. This is necessary for brevity. Their purpose is to illustrate points of general significance. The numbers indicate the chapters to which they are relevant.

3a If an insect has equal numbers of males and females, and each female lays on average 160 eggs, what rate of juvenile mortality would be required to prevent an upward or downward drift of abundance?

What must the above mortality become if the sex ratio is 55 per cent females?

3b If a population were reduced to the same number each winter by a limited food supply, increasing again 10-fold each spring, what percentage mortality could be inflicted in the summer without reducing the numbers surviving to the following spring? What could this summer mortality be if the spring increase were (i) 5-fold or (ii) 50-fold?

3c Suppose that a population of animals suffers 50 per cent mortality as it develops to maturity and that each surviving female lays 50 eggs all on the 20th day of its life, half of them female. What would be its (multiplicative) rate of increase per day, and per week? Compare the effects on the rate of increase of (a) halving the mortality, (b) doubling the number of eggs, and (c) halving the developmental period.

4a Here are three examples in which the numbers killed by a mortality factor differ according to population density:

Density		50	100	200	500	1000
Deaths caused	case 1:	1	3	20	200	900
by mortality	case 2:	13	32	58	175	300
factor in	case 3:	15	29	40	70	80

Draw graphs to show how the percentages killed are related to density in each case, and so identify the type of density-relationship involved.

Make up a further example of each of the three types of relationship.

4b On graph paper, make an approximate copy of Fig. 4–3, smoothing out the minor fluctuations. Then plot numbers of predators against numbers of hosts, reading the values from your graph at half-monthly intervals along the time scale; rule lines to link successive points.

5a Tabulate the classifications in §5.1, with two or three columns for each, then write the examples given (or other examples), in a list on the left, and tick the columns appropriate to each example.

5b   Suppose the graph line in Fig. 5–1 fell in position A, or in position B, what would be its biological interpretation? Write the equation for each line, also for the lines in Figs. 4–5 and 4–7.

6a   The data in Fig. 6–2 are as follows. Seeds sown per pot: 1, 5, 50, 100, 200. Seeds produced per plant that grew from the sown seeds and re-produced: 23,741; 6102; 990; 451; 210. Surface area of soil in pot, 182·5 sq. cm. Is the curve in Fig. 6–2 a hyperbola? Test this by plotting seed production per reproducing plant against the *reciprocal* of sowing density, i.e. space per seed planted: do the points fall along a straight line? Also, re-plot Fig. 6–2 on logarithmic scales. Draw a straight line as well as possible through the points in each graph and write down the equation of the line. Consider possible biological interpretations.

References

Books or papers marked * are recommended for general reading. Others deal with specific points referred to in the text or in the captions to illustrations or tables.

*ALLEE, W. C., EMERSON, A. E., PARK, O., PARK, T. and SCHMIDT, K. P. (1949). *Principles of Animal Ecology*. W. B. Saunders Co., Philadelphia and London.

*ANDREWARTHA, H. G. (1961). *Introduction to the Study of Animal Populations*. Methuen, London.

*ANDREWARTHA, H. G. and BIRCH, L. C. (1954). *The Distribution and Abundance of Animals*. University of Chicago Press, Chicago.

ASPINALL, D. and MILTHORPE, F. L. (1959). *Ann. appl. Biol.*, **47**, 156–72.

BURNETT, T. (1958a). *Can. Ent.*, **90**, 279–83.

BURNETT, T. (1958b). *Proc. Xth Int. Congr. Entom.* (Montreal, 1956), **2**, 679–86.

CHAPMAN, R. N. (1931). *Animal Ecology, with Especial Reference to Insects*. McGraw-Hill, New York.

*CLARK, L. R., GEIER, P. W., HUGHES, R. D., and MORRIS, R. F. (1967). *The Ecology of Populations in Theory and Practice*. Methuen, London.

CLATWORTHY, J. N. and HARPER, J. L. (1962). *J. exper. Bot.*, **13**, 307–24.

*DeBACH, PAUL (Ed.) (1964). *Biological Control of Insect Pests and Weeds*. Chapman & Hall, London.

DONALD, C. M. (1961). Pp. 282–313 in *Mechanisms in Biological Competition*. Edited by MILTHORPE, F. L. University Press, Cambridge.

*ELTON, CHARLES S. (1958). *The Ecology of Invasions by Animals and Plants*. Methuen, London.

HAMMOND, J. (1955). Pp. 113–20 in *The Numbers of Man and Animals*. Edited by CRAGG, J. B. and PIRIE, N. W. Oliver and Boyd, Edinburgh and London.

*HARDY, SIR ALISTER (1959). *The Open Sea: Its Natural History, Part II, Fish and Fisheries*. Collins, London.

HARPER, J. L. (1960). Pp. 119–32 in *The Biology of Weeds*. Edited by HARPER, J. L. Blackwell, Oxford.

HARPER, J. L. and MCNAUGHTON, I. H. (1962). *New Phytol.*, **61**, 175–88.

HOLLING, C. S. (1959a). *Can. Ent.*, **91**, 293–320.

HOLLING, C. S. (1959b). *Can. Ent.*, **91**, 385–98.

HOLLING, C. S. (1963). *Mem. Entom. Soc. Canada*, No. **32**, 22–32.

HOLLING, C. S. (1964). *Can. Ent.*, **96**, 335–47.

HUSSEY, N. W., PARR, W. J. and GOULD, H. J. (1965). *Ent. exp. appl.*, **8**, 271–81.

*LACK, D. (1966). *Population Studies of Birds*. Clarendon Press, Oxford.

LAMBERT, J. M. (Ed.) (1967). *The Teaching of Ecology*. Blackwell, Oxford and Edinburgh.

*LEWIS, T. and TAYLOR, L. R. (1967). *Introduction to Experimental Ecology*. Academic Press, London and New York.

*MacARTHUR, R. and CONNELL, J. (1966). *The Biology of Populations*. Wiley, New York, London and Sydney.

*MACFADYEN, A. (1963). *Animal Ecology. Aims and Methods*. Pitman, London.

MILTHORPE, F. L. (1961). Pp. 330–55 in *Mechanisms in Biological Competition*. Edited by MILTHORPE, F. L. University Press, Cambridge.

MORRIS, R. F. (1957). *Can. Ent.*, **89**, 49–69.

MORRIS, R. F. (1963). *Mem. Entom. Soc. Canada*, No. **32**, 16–21.

NEWTON, I. (1967). *J. Anim. Ecol.*, **36**, 721–44.

*NICHOLSON, A. J. (1954). *Aust. J. Zool.*, **2**, 9–65.

NICHOLSON, A. J. and BAILEY, V. A. (1935). *Proc. zool. Soc. Lond.*, **3**, 551–98.

NORRIS, J. R. (1965). *Ann. appl. Biol.*, **56**, 335.

ODUM, E. P. (1959). *Fundamentals of Ecology*. Saunders, Philadelphia and London.

PALMBLAD, I. G. (1968). *Ecology*, **49**, 26–34.

*PARK, T. (1955). Pp. 69–84 in *The Numbers of Man and Animals*. Edited by CRAGG, J. B. and PIRIE, N. W. Oliver and Boyd, Edinburgh and London.

PARK, T. (1962). *Science, N.Y.* **138**, 1369–75.

*PHILLIPSON, J. (1966). *Ecological Energetics*. Arnold, London.

*RICHARDS, O. W. (1958). The study of natural populations of insects. *Proc. R. Ent. Soc. Lond.*, Ser. C., **23**, 75–9.

RUSSELL, SIR JOHN (1954). *World Population and World Food Supplies*. Allen and Unwin, London.

SAGAR, G. R. and HARPER, J. L. (1961). *Weed Res.*, **1**, 163–76.

SOLOMON, M. E. (1964). *Adv. Ecol. Res.*, **2**, 1–58. Edited by CRAGG, J. B. Academic Press.

*SOUTHWOOD, T. R. E. (1966). *Ecological Methods*. Methuen, London.

*SOUTHWOOD, T. R. E. (Ed.) (1968). *Insect Abundance*. Blackwell, Oxford and Edinburgh.

VARLEY, G. C. and GRADWELL, G. R. (1960). *J. Anim. Ecol.*, **29**, 399–401.

VARLEY, G. C. and GRADWELL, G. R. (1968). Pp. 132–42 in *Insect Abundance*. Edited by SOUTHWOOD, T. R. E. Blackwell, Oxford and Edinburgh.

*WATERHOUSE, D. F. and WILSON, FRANK (1968). *Science Journal*, **4**, 31–7.

WATT, A. S. (1955). *J. Ecol.*, **43**, 490–506.

WHITTINGTON, W. J. and O'BRIEN, T. A. (1968). *J. appl. Ecol.*, **5**, 209–13.

WILLIAMSON, M. H. (1967). Pp. 169–76 in *The Teaching of Ecology*. Edited by LAMBERT, J. M. Blackwell, Oxford and Edinburgh.

WYNNE-EDWARDS, V. C. (1962). *Animal Dispersion in Relation to Social Behaviour*. Oliver and Boyd, Edinburgh and London.